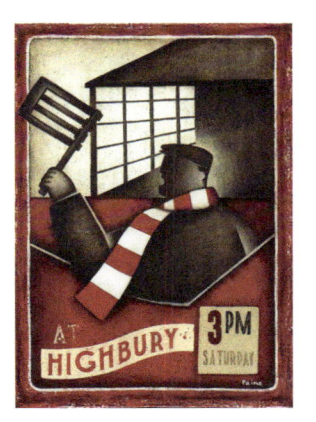

WE'VE ONLY GOT
ONE SONG
ARSENAL TERRACE SONGS & CHANTS

Published by
Legends Publishing

E-mail david@legendspublishing.net
Website www.legendspublishing.net

Copyright 2019

Notice of Rights
All rights reserved. Unless it is part of a published review, no part of this book may be reproduced or transmitted in any form or by any means, electronically or mechanical, including photocopying, recording, or by any other information storage and retrieval system, without prior written permission from the publisher. For information on getting permission for reprints and excerpts, contact Legends Publishing.

All views expressed in this book are the personal opinions of the individuals concerned and not necessarily those of the author, the publisher or the football club.

Any views expressed within songs in this book were the opinions of the crowd at the time, and not necessarily those of the authors, the publisher or the football club. All efforts have been made to ensure the content of this book is historically accurate but if any individual named feels they have been misrepresented your right to reply will be exercised if you so wish.

CONTENTS

INTRODUCTION	4
PLAYERS	9
OPPOSITION PLAYERS	42
SUPPORT	53
RIVALS	72
SPURS	82
ARSENAL AGGRO HELLO HELLO	98
PROTESTS & CONTROVERSY	109
COMEBACKS & CELEBRATIONS	125
PRE HIGHBURY	137
CONCLUSION	144
APPENDICES	149
SOURCES GENERAL	158

WE'VE ONLY GOT ONE SONG

INTRODUCTION

The theme of this book matters as much as any player biography. It matters as much as any statistic, record or pictorial history of Arsenal F.C. The culture that emanates from the crowd exemplifies the club as much as any individual, badge, shirt or building. They say football is nothing without fans; true, but football is boring without the right type of fans. Boring and incomplete without the supporters who create the noise, passion, humour and colour.

The fans are the club, because they're the one constant in a world where people move in and out of positions and jobs. On match day what happens within the crowd can sometimes be the saviour of an otherwise lacklustre afternoon. A dull draw, or a one sided cup win against lower league opposition can be brought to life by a single chant or an exchange of banter or insults between the rival fans. Just one amusing song directed at a player can be the one abiding memory from attending that game.

To use just one example, Matt has no significant memory of anything that happened on the pitch during a lifeless game between Arsenal and Newcastle in 1997. However, what he does remember from that game was a very clear and loud Clock End rendition of 'SHEARER'S A WANKER'.

Today, football is considered entertainment and the role of the crowd is to sit down and be entertained. Not everyone confirms, and nor should they, because English football, traditionally over the decades, has had a music hall and pantomime mentality; in that - a fundamental aspect is crowd participation; fun, banter, abuse, heroes, villains, and love of a good sing song. Unlike ballet and opera - music hall and pantomime do not work or fulfil their purpose unless the crowd does their bit for the show. The interaction between the performers and watchers is crucial as sport does not have a predefined ending, unlike a play.

How good, or bad, the crowd were that day has such an overwhelming and undervalued impact into the whole experience of attending a game. A great team performance can feel flat because the stadium was quiet and appeared vocally unappreciative of the performance. And vice versa.

The vocal passion of Arsenal supporters is a paradox in football fan culture. On the one hand, the majority of fans who populate the Emirates stadium are quiet and reserved when watching the game. They don't appear to know many songs, and at best they might join in with a rendition of:

"AND IT'S ARSENAL,
ARSENAL FC,
WE'RE BY FAR THE GREATEST TEAM,
THE WORLD HAS EVER SEEN!"
(Wild Rover)

Then in a local pub after, or indeed during the game, you'll hear a variety of songs and chants from people situated together in a free environment and rivalling any set of fans in England for passion and noise. The culture of football chants and songs could only be born out of groups standing together. Once the seats came in - things got quieter; but the pubs managed to keep the football song alive. The pub is the origin of most football chants. This is where songs are thought of, tried out, and then maybe even heard in the stadium.

Songs that don't get sung in the stadium may still be included in this book as long they are used by Arsenal fans in pubs and other such venues. There is one criteria for a chant or song being included in this book: Arsenal fans, situated at any spot on planet Earth (and beyond) singing football related chants. The stadium, whilst the focus, is just one of thousands of venues where Arsenal fans watch the game.

Matthew Bazell started going to games in the mid to late 1980s as a Junior Gunner, while Mark Andrews started in 1978 and back then atmosphere, or lack of it, was not a relevant issue. It was in your hands what environment you wanted to be part of. If you wanted to sit down and watch the game - you had the East and West Stands. If you wanted a good sing song you went to the middle or top side of the North Bank terrace. If you wanted to have a song and 'dance' with the away fans you went to the Clock End.

Interestingly, while there are quite a few songs from the Plumstead era, there appear to be very few from World War One to the 1950s. While newspapers may have under reported songs in this period the dearth of tunes other than those sung at big occasions such as the communal FA cup singing does chime with other studies of crowds. In this period especially the 30s many supporters mainly sang pub songs and other ditties within their own peer group of mates, and were localised on the terraces.

We would have enjoyed finding some inter-war songs from the terraces but these just did not reveal themselves, and certainly there was little to nothing of the continuous singing and chanting that typified the contemporary game.

However, the variety and breadth of songs from the 1960s onwards was translated into a different terrace experience, as youth culture exploded. A good intelligent reworking of a favourite tune with witty words that scanned was quickly picked up by the rest of the crowd.

Arsenal songs over the years follow the same pattern of most English clubs, in that church hymns, seaside songs and music hall favourites were the most used pieces of music copied, and in many cases corrupted. In the last decade or two it's more common for chants to be to the rhymes of modern pop music; modern including the 1960s as the Beach Boys classic 'Sloop John

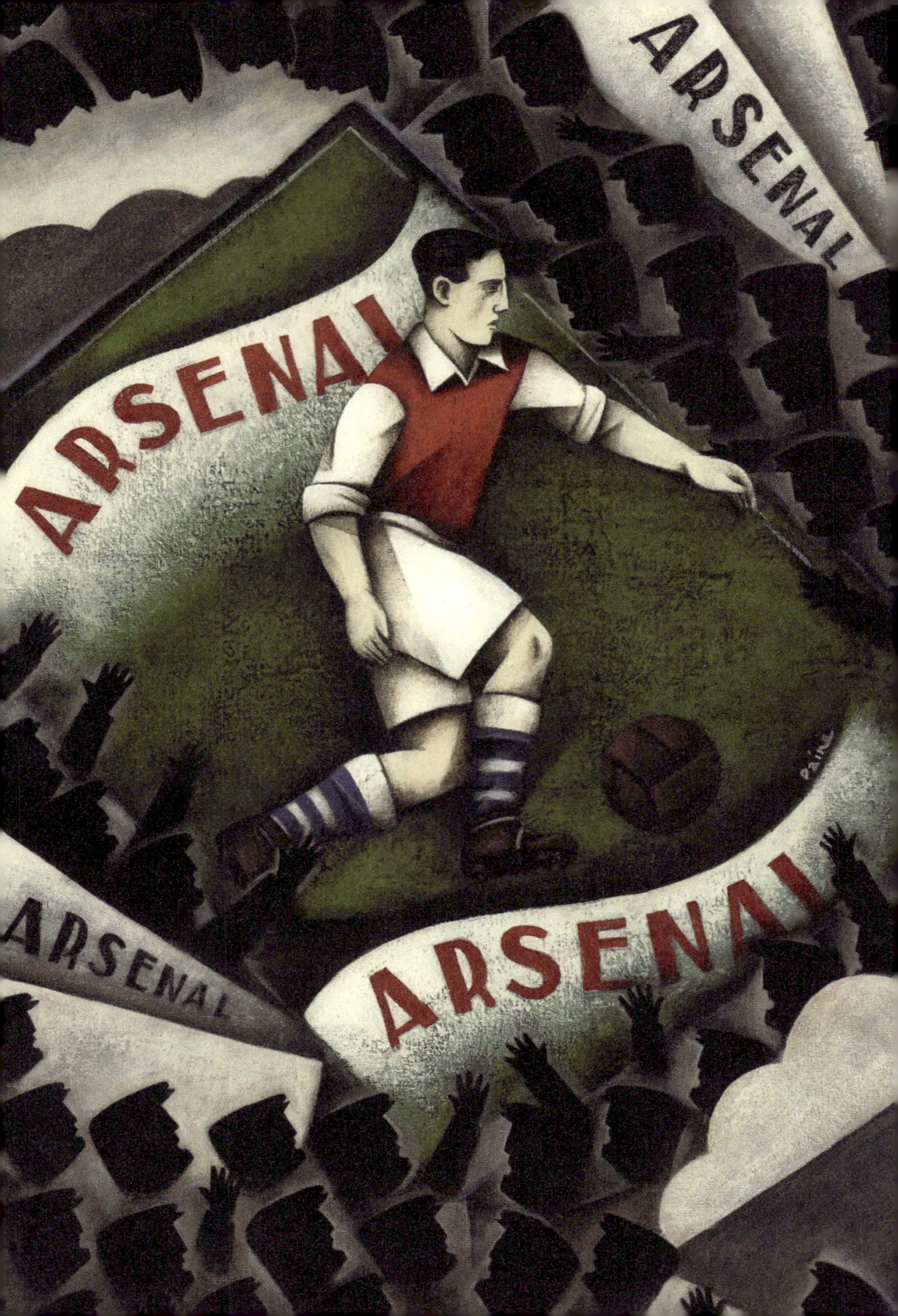

ARSENAL
ARSENAL
ARSENAL
ARSENAL

B' is by far the most common song used to create new football chants in the 21st Century. Too commonly used some might say - 2016/17 onwards, the 1990s Billy Ray Cyrus song 'Achy Breaky Heart' is rapidly, and disturbingly, becoming overused in football stadiums!

During the production and publication of 'We've Only Got One Song' more chants have been created along with hundreds more in the coming years. Long may it continue, and for what this book has the ability and means to cover, we hope all Arsenal fans enjoy the memories that they created.

This is not meant to be a full and formal encyclopaedia of chants, but a light hearted look at the multitude of Arsenal songs over the years. There may be some that you can recall that we have not included, but there will be plenty that you do recognise and hopefully will bring back good memories. One of the intrigues we hope this book will bring is the coming across of chants that you've never heard before - or ones that you would not have associated with Arsenal supporters.

Whilst writing, a smirk or smile of recognition of long forgotten chants passed both our faces, and indeed a specific location remembered when a song was sung. For many, Highbury will be the location they remember, and in particular the North Bank or Clock End, as that was where the majority of these tunes were aired.

One definition of a chant is that it can be a phrase or slogan repeated rhythmically and insistently, with or without a tune, such as "COME ON YOU REDS". Whereas a song has melody is more lyrical with verses and a chorus, such as "SHE WORE A YELLOW RIBBON".

As chanting in unison within a crowd has the same effect as singing we are treating both the same and make no distinction between the two words which will be used interchangeably. At a football match sometimes a song is more effective, and on another occasion a chant.

We discussed a method of presenting each song within each chapter. Would we go for an alphabetical arrangement, a chronological one or other criteria. We went for none of those: we have mainly gone for a random selection. Much like the spontaneous and apparently unstructured chants that emanated from terraces we have placed them anywhere we fancied. As a song came into our heads it was then randomly inserted into the most appropriate chapter.

The club has a reputation for having a quiet fan base, but reputations don't always represent reality. Over the years Arsenal fans have created incredible atmospheres and come up with some of the funniest and creative chants and songs; of which there are too many to cover in one book, but most of the best ones are in here.

Despite the relative lack of noise in the current era, there are plenty of memories, and as long as there are Arsenal fans there will be more chants and songs to remember in the coming years. This is a celebration of over 100 years of supporting the team we love - and this book is dedicated to every single Arsenal fan who has ever sung in support for the team. This is your book.

Disclaimer

All the chants and songs featured in this book are genuine chants which have been obtained from the various sources as noted in the bibliography and acknowledgements.

We apologise if any offence is taken by any of our readers as many of these songs contain bad language. They may be sexist, violent, homophobic or just insulting Tottenham.

They are included here simply to ensure the completeness of the record and their publication in no way condones such sentiments.

Please note that there's a lot of irreverence with football songs, and they are not meant to be taken overly seriously.

Mores and societal consent regarding certain words or phrases has changed over time. This is primarily a historical book and as such documents songs, some aspects of which over time have become verboten or just plain unacceptable to many modern ears.

Many are not heard anymore due firstly to the increased vigilance of the police who were empowered to arrest people making racial remarks or taunts. Secondly, fans themselves became more aware of the inappropriateness of such chants, and this has occurred at different periods over the years with racial, anti-semitic, homophobic and more latterly sexist chants.

We are not going to utilise any overtly or covert racist chants or songs with overtones of genocide. Whilst very few in number these were disgraceful then, as they still are.

If material of this nature is likely to offend you, or you are under 16 years of age then please do not proceed further. We ask that if you're likely to take offence don't purchase or even look at this book.

Acknowledgements

Kelvin 'Singer' Meadows: for putting us right on many songs, and an incredible font of terrace knowledge. Similarly Gary Lawrence: for loads of 1960s and 1970s songs. Andy Kelly for sage advice, all statistics via www.thearsenalhistory.com and Steve Murphy for proof reading.

Davy Boyd @boyd_d1; Gav @shewore; G @Northbank1968; Nicholas Andrews; Lee Gregory; Mark King; Glen Townsend; Craig Cooper; Darren Berry, The Laughing Gooner, Highbury Harold @blackscarfafc, Michael 'Binsey' Joyce and TP for a series of inspired comments, insight and songs.

To all Herdsmen who responded to the website for our request for songs. Ammer, an old North Bank boy and Barry Dixey who also stood on the North Bank Terraces for many years.

And last, and by no means least, thanks to the remarkable artistic talent of Paine Proffit for his excellent Arsenal player paintings, and for granting his permission to use his artwork in this book.

PLAYERS

Going to games in the years of open terracing, for many people, meant getting into the ground an hour before kick-off, in order to get to your normal location, or best spot. During this time the players would warm up in front of thousands of people and the atmosphere before the game would usually be pretty good. Not to say that every pre-match was like this but many, many were.

This would lead to players having chants directed at them and virtually everyone was acknowledged.

This pre-game staple was the notion of chants for most players in order of seniority / skill / value to the team. So in the late 1970s Brady would be first, then O'Leary, Alan Sunderland, Young, Rice, and so on.

Each player would then applaud the crowd in turn on hearing their song. It is sad that the link between fans and players has been broken by the Premier League/TV money combination and all it entails. Since the introduction of the seats the culture of player chants remained but does not occur prior to games anymore.

"ONE SONG, WE'VE ONLY GOT ONE SONG."
(Blue Moon)

A simple yet brilliant ode for midfielder Alex Song (2005-2012) a mercurial player who left after 204 games - for the bench at Barcelona.

This chant was not just for Song, it was also a twist on the derogatory chant 'ONE SONG, YOU'VE ONLY GOT ONE SONG" aimed at quiet crowds, or crowds who only ever apparently sing one song.

"WE'VE ONLY GOT ONE JUAN."
(Blue Moon)

In February 2002 at home to the Gills in the FA cup for Juan, our left back received this ditty. This game only his second was also was his swansong!

**"HIS NAME IS SILVA, GILBERTO SILVA,
HE'S ARSENAL'S BRAZILIAN MIDFIELDER."**
(Copa Cabana by Barry Manilow)

WE'VE ONLY GOT ONE SONG

This song for Gilberto (2002-2008) was not heard in stadiums, and we didn't even know it existed until we researched it. Maybe people just didn't want to be seen singing a Barry Manilow song? Despite being a reliable regular during a very successful period, Gilberto's name wasn't being sung in the stands even though he was solid, respected and liked. The same applied to defender Lauren (2000-2007) who was a fellow 'Invincible'. He had a song but very rarely heard:

"LAUREN, LAU-REN,
LAUREN, LAU-REN,
LAUREN, LAUREN, LAUREN,
LAUREN!"
(My Gang [come on, come on] by Gary Glitter – very unfortunate!)

"HE JUST WANTS A SONG (Repeat once)
LAURENT KOSCIELNY
HE JUST WANTS A SONG."
(Sloop John B)

Laurent Koscielny (2010 to 2019) was going the same way as Gilberto and Lauren and had no popular ode to his name. He took action and stated his desire to have a chant like all his team mates. Gilberto and Lauren – all you had to do was ask!

"AIN'T NOBODY, LIKE KOSCIELNY,
MAKES ME HAPPY,
MAKES ME FEEL THIS WAY,
AIN'T NOBODY LIKE KOSCIELNY AND GIR-OOOOUD."
(Ain't Nobody)

Outside a pub in Zagreb before the Champions League game in 2015 this Chaka Khan classic was used to give Koscielny a proper song, though even then he did not have it all to himself and had to share it with Giroud! Bearing in mind Koscielny's recent sour departure, and Giroud's post Baku final antics, we have to ask was this song worth it?

"TORREIRA OH, OH, OH, OH, (Repeat once)
HE COMES FROM URUGUAY,
HE'S ONLY FIVE FOOT HIGH,
TORREIRA OH, OH, OH, OH. (Repeat once)
(Volare - Dean Martin)

It's only fair to Torreira to say that officially his height is stated as 5ft 6 in.

"AUBAMEYANG, DER, DER, DER, DER, DER!
AUBAMEYANG, DER, DER, DER, DER, DER!"
(Muppets' theme tune)

**"DO, DO, DO, DO, DO, ALEX LACAZETTE,
DO, DO, DO, DO, DO, ALEX LACAZETTE."**
(This Girl - Kungs vs Cookin' on 3 Burners)

In a seemingly bizarre twist, Lacazette gets a rousing, gutteral chant, based upon a hook in the splendid 2016 Franco-Australian dance-floor hit. Whilst his striking partner, Aubameyang, has been allocated the Muppet's theme.

"AUBAMEYANG, "AUBAMEYANG, "AUBAMEYANG!" (Repeat often)

However, this has been rectified particularly in the recent Europa League semi final at Valencia, as a magnificent hat-trick led the away end to repeatedly sing a different chant for him. A suitable upgrade for the golden boot winner of 2019.

**"STEVE BOULD (Repeat once)
STEVIE, STEVIE, BOULD,
HE'S GOT NO HAIR,
BUT WE DON'T CARE,
STEVIE, STEVIE BOULD."**
(Hooray Hooray It's a Holi-Holiday – Bonney M)

Steve Bould (1988-1999) one of the legendary members of George Graham's defensive unit had a more complex song compared to other defencive player chants at Arsenal. When he arrived he had a bit of hair but after a few seasons he became more challenged on the follicle front, and this song was born.

Bould arrived from Stoke, appeared in 372 matches and won a host of trophies before finishing his career at Sunderland. Bould's team mates had chants, but it was mostly their name being chanted and nothing else. For example the legendary unit's two full backs only words in their chants were:–

"LEE DIXON, LEE DIXON, LEE DIXON." (repeat)
(Stars and Stripes Forever)

"NIGEL WINTERBURN, NIGEL WINTERBURN." (repeat)
(Chirpy Chirpy Cheep Cheep)

Nigel Winterburn (1987-2000) and Lee Dixon (1988-2002), were both, like Bould, purchased from smaller clubs to form a unit with Tony Adams. Dixon who arrived with Bould from Stoke also won many medals and played in 619 games before retiring from playing as an Arsenal player.

Winterburn arrived from Wimbledon, appearing 584 times for the Gunners and also gained a host of winners medals, before ending his career at the West Ham retirement home.

**ADAMS IN UNEXPECTED HORIZONTAL ACTION
AGAINST NOTTINGHAM FOREST IN NOVEMBER 1988**

With the number of appearances these defenders put in, you would have thought they would have had better songs, but there you are.

**"THERE'S ONLY ONE TONY ADAMS,
ONE TONY ADAMS
THERE'S ONLY ONE TONY ADAMS,
ONE TONY ADAMS." (repeat)**
(Guantanamera)

or

"OOH OOH TONY ADAMS."
(Chant)

Tony Adams (1983-2002) the longest serving Arsenal captain of all time, immortalised by the club with a statue and centre back colossus, did initially have a slight upgrade on the full backs.

**"WE'VE LOST TONY ADAMS
OH TONY ADAMS
WE'VE LOST TONY ADAMS
AND HE'S GONE, GONE, GONE
OH, OH, OH, OH"**
(Lost That Loving Feeling)

Aston Villa away - a few days prior to Xmas day 1990 was the first game Arsenal played after captain Tony Adams was sentenced to four months in prison for drunk-driving. Not long before the jail term, he had made headlines for sticking two fingers up at QPR fans (nothing wrong with that) as well as a sending off at Luton. It was a bleak time for Adams, and along with two docked points from the FA, Arsenal winning the title looked like an up-hill struggle.

Adams returned in late February and drew thousands of fans to a reserve game against Reading at Highbury, who came to support and forgive him. In May 1991 he lifted the league title trophy for the champions who lost only one game all season.

"DAVID O'LEARY (clap clap clap clap clap)
DAVID O'LEARY
DAVID O'LEARY" (Repeated)
(Chant)

This very basic chant also had a bizarre derivation which rather than sing his name "David O'Leary" - just went "der der, der der der" which worked phonetically. So much so that was what many remember just singing - not his name.

David O'Leary (1973-1993) Arsenal's record appearance holder, with 722 games, began as an apprentice in 1973, was then pretty much an automatic starter from his debut in 1975 until 1989. A classic central defender, he was captain for a while in the early 1980s, and made his final bow for the Gunners in the 1993 FA Cup final replay victory. While O'Leary started in the 1970s this was still being sung for him in the 1990s.

"SOLS A GOONER, DER DER DER DER DER."
(Papa's Got a Brand New Pig Bag)

Similar to the David O'Leary chant from the 1970s-1990s, but with a modern twist.

"KEOWN, KEOWN, KEOWN"
(Chant)

More of a chant than a song, and similar to Theo Walcott's chant of;

"THEO, THEO, THEO"
(Chant)

"HE'S TALL,
HE'S SHIT,
HE PLAYS WHEN NO-ONE'S FIT,
BIG CYGAN, BIG CYGAN,
HE'S SHIT,
HE'S FRENCH,

**HE'S ALWAYS ON THE BENCH,
BIG CYGAN, BIG CYGAN!"**
(In The Quarter Master's Store)

When Pascal Cygan (2002-2006) joined Arsenal, the club had a reputation for having formidable centre backs of the highest quality. Tony Adams, Steve Bould and David O'Leary were three legends who had left Highbury, but Martin Keown was still there along with Sol Campbell who was a recent addition to the roster.

Cygan, despite being an 'Invincible', gained a reputation for being clumsy, and someone who could only possibly be risked in the team if everyone else was injured. He left having also picked up two FA cup winners medals. Some may say these were won despite him. But certainly as the quality of the central defence decreased - the song complexity increased!

**"IGORS STEPANOVS,
TRA-LA-LA-LA-LA"**
(Brown Girl in the Ring)

Latvian Igors Stepanovs (2000-2003) made 31 appearances for the club, and it is beyond comprehension how he got a good song, and how anyone thought that 'Brown Girl in the Ring' was a fitting theme.

It is also hard to comprehend that according to Ray Parlour he was only purchased after a training pitch prank by the team on Martin Keown that Arsene Wenger misconstrued.

**"HE CAME TO US WHEN HENRY LEFT,
EDDIE, EDDIE,
HE SCORES MORE GOALS THAN DARREN BENT,
EDDIE, EDDIE,
HE BROKE HIS LEG, BUT HE'LL BE BACK,
AND DARREN BENT WILL STILL BE CAK,
EDUARDO SILVA, ARSENAL'S NUMBER 9"**
(The Animals Came Marching in)

After an utterly horrific leg break at Birmingham in February 2008, Eduardo Da Silva (2007-10) scored on his comeback game at Highbury against Cardiff in February 2009. After 67 appearances he was sold to Shakhtar Donetsk in 2010 and returned to the Emirates Stadium for a Champions League tie in October of that year. Arsenal led 5-0 before the highlight of the night, a consolation goal from 'Eddie' for his new team which was greeted with cheers from the home crowd.

**"HE CAME TO US WHEN BENDTNER LEFT,
CHU YOUNG, CHU YOUNG
AND NOT A LOT OF CASH WAS SPENT,
CHU YOUNG, CHU YOUNG,**

**GIVE HIM THE BALL AND HE WILL SCORE,
DON'T LET HIM WALK YOUR LABRADOR,
PARK CHU YOUNG, THE ARSENAL NUMBER 9"**
(The Animals Came Marching in)

South Korean Park Chu Young (2011-2014) has a record at Arsenal of seven games and one goal - and was probably bought in to sell Arsenal shirts in Seoul, as he was popular in his home country. He spent much of his three season Arsenal spell on loan for Spanish club Celta Viga and then Watford.

"IAN WRIGHT, WRIGHT, WRIGHT"
(Feeling Hot Hot Hot)

This was a slight deviation from just the name that players such as Alan Smith or Niall Quinn heard. The song was a 1980s and 1990s hit for a number of artistes and the annotation of "Alan, Smith, Smith, Smith" didn't quite have the same ring.

Ian Wright (1991-1998) arrived from Crystal Palace in September 1991 and went onto score 185 goals in 288 games, and in the process beating Cliff Bastin's club goal scoring record which had stood since before World War Two started. Wright left for the West Ham retirement home in the summer after the 1997-98 Double win.

Since he finished playing, he has become a gloriously unpredictable TV commentator at games, except for one factor: his obvious and absolute love for the Gunners and England which steadily shines through.

"RICHARD WRIGHT, WRIGHT, WRIGHT!"
(Feeling Hot Hot Hot)

After Ian Wright left his chant morphed into one for Richard Wright (2001-2002). Wright a one season wonder arrived from Ipswich and left for Everton in between helping the Gunners to a League and FA Cup double. Though unable to oust Seaman from the number one role, he played 22 times keeping seven clean sheets for the Arsenal.

**"A MAN CAME UP, TO ME ONE NIGHT,
HE SAID HE'S SEEN, THE NEW IAN WRIGHT,
I SAID TO HIM, WHO CAN THAT BE,
AND HE SAID TO ME, THIERRY HENRY,
THIERRY HENRY" (Repeat multiple times)**
(Tom Hark by the Piranhas)

Thierry Henry (1999-2007 & 2012) – 228 goals in 377 games, passed Ian Wright's record in November 2005 - nuff said.

FRANK
McLINTOCK
A
F
C
70
71
1964
1973
THE LEAGUE LEADER - F.A. CUP 70-71
Paine

**"HIS NAME IS ALAN SMITH AND HE'S THE LEADER OF OUR TEAM,
THE GREATEST CENTRE FORWARD, THE WORLD HAS EVER SEEN,
HE'S HERE, HE'S THERE, HE'S EVERYWHERE,
HE SCORES THE VITAL GOAL,
AND AS FOR IAN RUSH, YOU CAN STICK HIM UP YOUR HOLE"**
(McNamara's band)

Sung in the Wat Tyler pub at Dartford in the late 1980s and early 1990s by Davy Boyd and the Arsenal crew who frequented this Kentish watering hole. Alan Smith (1987-1995), is a two time golden boot winner and scored 115 goals in 347 games for Arsenal. He may just go down as one of the most underappreciated legends of recent history; which was maybe down to him being eclipsed by Ian Wright. Smith was vital in the successes of the George Graham era, scoring the first goal of Anfield 89 and the winning goal in the 1994 European Cup Winners Cup final; at the time of writing the only European success the club has had between 1970 and the present. A quite shocking record for one of the biggest clubs in Europe. And speaking of Anfield 89:

"THERE'S ONLY ONE MICHAEL THOMAS"
(Guantemamera)

And indeed there was after the incredible 1989 finale. His name was sung long and loud as the bus moved around Islington on the Sunday after the Friday before.

Michael Thomas (1982-1991) signed as a schoolboy in September 1982 and worked his way through the ranks before his debut in February 1987. He scored 30 times in 208 games before moving to Liverpool in December 1991, the irony of his most important goal being scored against his new employers was commented upon by many supporters. Though he did not want to leave, he was sold after apparent disagreements with George Graham.

"FRANKIE MCLINTOCK" (clap, clap, clap, clap, clap)

Another in the line of players with just their name as the chant, and given his pedigree certainly deserved more. Arguably the finest Arsenal captain in modern times; an honour he would fight out with Tony Adams, Frank McLintock (1964-1973) skippered the side for six seasons from 1967 to 1973. He was the man who lifted the FA cup and League Championship Trophy double in 1971, as well as the UEFA Fairs Cup a year earlier.

Signed from Leicester in October 1964 he was a steely mainstay in defence until sold to QPR in June 1973, having made 403 appearances for the club.

Latterly he formed one half of a comedy double act with old teammate Eddie Kelly while helping to promote David Seager's George Armstrong book in 2015. A true gentleman and proper Gunner.

> "CHARLIE GEORGE,
> SUPERSTAR,
> HOW MANY GOALS,
> HAVE YOU SCORED SO FAR?"
> (Jesus Christ Superstar)

A regular cry from the Arsenal crowd in the early 1970s when Charlie scored. However it was easily countered by the opposing support, as we show in the next chapter.

> "CHARLIE... CHARLIE... CHARLIE... CHARLIE,
> BORN IS THE KING OF HIGHBURY"
> (Noel)

Charlie George (1966-1975) surely wins the argument for 'the most Arsenal man to have ever played for the club.' He grew up in Highbury and supported Arsenal. He watched from the terraces; the Laundry End which was renamed the North Bank around the time he signed on schoolboy terms. He helped put up the boxing ring at Highbury for Ali-Cooper. He became one of the greatest attacking players in Arsenal history and helped the club win their first European trophy. He won the league and cup double scoring the winning goal in the FA Cup final, one of the 49 goals he scored for the Gunners.

George played in 179 Arsenal games which was a ridiculously low total for one so talented, but injuries and disagreements with authority, especially Bertie Mee, took their toll. Famous for his interaction with opponent crowds courtesy of the 'Harvey Smith' V sign, he left for Derby, where he is similarly popular, but remained in the Arsenal crowd's hearts.

After retirement he still attended games home and away. He currently makes a living as a guide for stadium tour events at Ashburton Grove. Charlie George – King of Arsenal.

> "WHERE DID HE COME FROM?
> HE WAS BORN IN A FLAT IN HOLLOWAY,
> HE'LL PLAY FOR ENGLAND ONE FINE DAY?
> YES HE WILL,
> I KNOW HE WILL,
> OH CHARLIE, OH CHARLIE,
> WHAT DID HE DO?
> HE SCORED TWO GOALS AT MAN CITY,
> HE SCORED THE WINNER AT WEMBLEY,
> HE LEADS US ON TO VICTORY,
> OH CHARLIE! OH CHARLIE!"
> (Any Old Iron)

And Charlie George did play for England one fine day – but no other day. He retired, albeit after telling manager Don Revie to 'stick it', with only one England appearance to his name and is cited as one of many 'England Mavericks' who were shunned by the 1970s high brow England FA establishment. Incredible players in this era were given the cold shoulder and Charlie George is part of a list of unused talent which most notably also included Tony Currie, Frank Worthington, Alan Hudson and Rodney Marsh. English football was blessed with second to none talent, yet the national team never qualified for the 1974 or 1978 World Cups.

"RADFORD FOR ENGLAND!"
(Chant)

A long forgotten chant which was always followed by some brisk clapping. It could involve any player who was performing well at the time, such as Jon Sammels, Ray Kennedy, Bob McNab or those criminally neglected by England such as George Armstrong or Peter Simpson. A few decades later it was reprised in a joking fashion for Perry Groves.

Arsenal's current fourth highest ever scorer with 149 goals John Radford (1962-76), actually played twice for England to add to his 482 Gunners performances.

The song is now long forgotten because firstly: the Premier League era has seen the importing of many non British players, and secondly playing for your country appears less of an honour to super rich players these days, and consequently no longer the pinnacle they strive for. It's more common now for fans to moan about their team's players being called up for the national squad, in case they get injured or a bit tired.

**"OB LA DI, OB LA DA, JOHNNY RADFORD,
JOHNNY RADFORD IS THE KING!
JOHNNY TAKES ARSENAL TO THE TOP OF THE LEAGUE,
WINS A TWENTY CARAT GOLD CUP,
TAKES IT BACK TO BERTIE WAITING ON THE BANK,
AND AS HE SHOWS IT TO THEM THEY BEGIN TO SING,
OB LA DI, OB LA DA, JOHNNY RADFORD,
JOHNNY RADFORD IS THE KING!"**
(Ob la di ob la da – The Beatles)

A song that was penned by Lennon and McCartney, but made popular in England by Marmalade whose cover of this Beatles track hit the top of the charts in January 1969.

The North Bank showed their appreciation of this remarkably catchy tune with the veneration of rugged forward John Radford, just in time for the Fairs Cup win, and then the Double.

If we had a time machine we would love to have been on the North Bank to hear that being sung on a sunny day during the 1970-71 season.

Now as often happens with what is essentially an oral history; that is where the information is passed down by word of mouth not on paper; many of these songs are not recorded but are present in the memories of those who were there. We have picked up two versions of this particular song, quite similar but not the same.

> "OB LA DI, OB LA DA, JOHNNY RADFORD,
> JOHNNY RADFORD IS OUR KING
> HAPPY EVER AFTER AT THE TOP OF THE LEAGUE
> FOUR AND TWENTY CARAT GOLDEN CUP
> TAKE IT BACK TO BERTIE WAITING AT THE DOOR
> AND AS HE GIVES IT TO HIM HE BEGINS TO SING
> "OB LA DI OB LA DA JOHNNY RADFORD,
> JOHNNY RADFORD IS OUR KING

What we believe this shows is that on the massed ranks of the North Bank some people would have been singing one and a few others a slightly different version, but that would have been masked by the overall singing to the same tune. Much like as a schoolchild singing different lyrics to the hymns at assembly. Or mishearing some words on your favourite pop song and assuming a quite different lyric.

> "HERE'S TO YOU JIMMY ROBERTSON
> ARSENAL LOVES YOU MORE THAN YOU WILL KNOW
> WOE WOE WOE"
> (Mrs Robinson)

A Scottish International, Jimmy Robertson (1968-1970) was signed from Tottenham, playing 59 times for the Gunners for two seasons before leaving for Ipswich. His arrival at Highbury co-incidentally just after the Graduate soundtrack tune "Mrs Robinson" was released as a top 10 number in the hit parade, allowed the North Bank to celebrate him in style.

> "COME ON WITHOUT
> COME ON WITHIN
> YOU'LL NOT SEE NOTHING LIKE THE MIGHTY JIM"
> (The Mighty Quinn)

Goalkeeper Jim 'Fingers' Furnell (1963-1968) was sandwiched in time between the sticks by two Arsenal greats: Jack Kelsey and Bob Wilson. Arriving from Liverpool, he made 167 appearances including the 1968 League Cup loss before leaving for Rotherham. The Mighty Quinn was no 1 in the hit parade in early 1968 forming a soundtrack for him as he kept goal in front of the North Bank.

> "SAMMELS, SAMMELS,
> I'D WALK A MILLION MILES,
> FOR ONE OF YOUR GOALS,
> JON SAMMELS"
> (Mammy by Al Jolson)

STOREY AND MCLINTOCK, EACH WITH A NICE CUP OF TEA, AWAIT THE FA HEARING IN JANUARY 1968

Sung from the mid-1960s as a tribute to the classy, goal scoring, midfielder who netted in the Highbury leg of the 1970 Fairs Cup Final. Though, ironically Sammels (1961-1971) a gifted skilful player who began at the club as an apprentice was eventually to give as his main reason for leaving the club as barracking from the Arsenal fans. Sammels played 270 times for the Gunners until he left for Leicester after picking up his League Championship winners medal in 1971.

**"PETER STOREY STEAMING IN,
STEAMING IN, STEAMING IN,
PETER STOREY STEAMING IN,
PETER STOREY!"**
(London Bridge is Falling Down)

Each team had a hatchet man in the 1970s: Tommy Smith represented Liverpool, Chelsea had "Chopper" Harris, Leeds had their whole team, and Arsenal had Peter Storey (1961-1977). The hard man's "hard man"; Storey went about his destroyer tasks with apparent relish, though he could also play constructively as befits a man who won 19 England caps.

Signed from school, he started out in the youth team and became a regular first team defender from 1965 onwards. He was moved from full back to defensive midfield in 1970 and he came into his own as a midfield battler loved on the North Bank, winning tackles, dumping opponents on their arse or simply fouling them. Though to be fair he was no slouch in previously carrying out these duties at full back.

Famously he held his bottle with a last minute penalty in the 1971 FA cup semi-final to keep the double dream alive. Surprisingly for such a combative and archetypal hard man he was only sent off twice as a Gunner in his 501 competitive appearances. There is little doubt that were he playing in today's game that figure would be exponentially higher.

His first was a double marching order with Frank McLintock at Burnley in December 1967, as Arsenal became the first side to have two players sent off during a match since World War Two, albeit in different episodes. According to the referee Storey was sent off as he proposed "a right old flow of language to describe referees in general and me in particular" McLintock only received a slapped wrist, but Storey was given a 14-day suspension from the FA for speaking his mind.

His second sending off in 1975 against Stoke - showed why he was so well liked by the support as he lived up to his 'Steaming In' chant by running a full 25 yards before kicking John Mahoney squarely in the back. This occurred in the 85th minute after a melee had formed around Alan Ball and Mahoney.

Storey was quoted in the Daily Express at the time: "Mahoney was having a go at Alan Ball and I went in to defend my team-mate. I suppose the referee was right to send me off but none of it would have happened if he had taken tougher action in the first place." On leaving the pitch Storey, who had history with Stoke particularly in 1971, had part of a brick thrown and punches aimed at him in an unpleasant precursor to the recent dislike between the two clubs.

**"WE'LL BE RUNNING ROUND WEMBLEY WITH THE CUP,
WE'LL BE RUNNING ROUND WEMBLEY WITH THE CUP,
WE'LL BE RUNNING ROUND WEMBLEY,
RUNNING ROUND WEMBLEY,
RUNNING ROUND WEMBLEY WITH THE CUP,
SINGING AYE AYE IAN IAN URE,
SINGING AYE AYE IAN IAN URE,
SINGING AYE AYE IAN,
AYE AYE IAN,
SINGING AYE AYE IAN IAN URE!"**
(She'll be coming round the mountain)

Sung in anticipation of a League Cup win in either 1968 or 1969, neither trip to Wembley was to prove fruitful for the team or for Ian Ure who appeared as centre back in both finals against Leeds and then Swindon.

Ian Ure (1963-1969) played 202 games for Arsenal at centre half, but a drop in form meant he left for Manchester United shortly after the League Cup final defeat against Swindon. He was last seen at Arsenal for the 100 club celebration of George Armstrong in late February 2016 where he came down to London from Scotland for his ex-colleague.

**"BOBBY GOULD VIVA BOBBY GOULD
BOBBY GOULD VIVA BOBBY GOULD VIVA VIVA (repeat)"**
(Viva Bobby Joe by the Equals)

Released in 1969 by the Equals, a band from Hornsey Rise led by a youthful Eddy Grant, it was as if this was made for Arsenal's forward who appeared 83 times for the club during a few seasons between 1968 and 1970. It was subsequently taken up by other team's fans with a Bobby in their side.

**"HE'S HERE,
HE'S THERE,
HE'S EVERY FUCKING WHERE,
BOBBY GOULD,
BOBBY GOULD!"**
(In The Quarter Master's Stores)

Bobby Gould also had this one in the late 1960s, and it was re-cycled by the North Bank for Charlie George into the 1970s.

**"HE SCORES GOALS WITH HIS RIGHT FOOT,
HE SCORES GOALS WITH HIS LEFT,
HE PLAYS ON THE WING FOR ARSENAL,
AND HE LOOKS LIKE GEORGIE BEST,
THEY CALL HIM MARINELLO,
PETER MARINELLO"**
(Mellow Yellow)

Talented Scotsman Peter Marinello (1970-1973) joined the club for £100,000; and the first Arsenal signing of six figures came with hope that he could be the next George Best. That expectation was exceeded when he scored on his Arsenal debut against Manchester United at Old Trafford. He had the appearance of George Best, but he let the same bad lifestyle choices ruin what could have been a great career.

Heavy drinking, partying and bad luck with injuries resulted in only 51 appearances and 5 goals in his Arsenal career. The song Mellow Yellow had been a hit in 1967 but its adoption for Marinello did not have the desired effect.

**"NA NA NA NA,
NA NA NA NA,
HEY HEY HEY,
MARINELLO "**
(Na Na Hey Hey (Kiss Him Goodbye)

This song was riding high in the charts in late 1969, and very soon afterwards Arsenal purchased Marinello from Hibernian. Initially a darling of the terraces, it was unfortunate that he did not live up to the colossal hype, eventually moving to Portsmouth.

WE'VE ONLY GOT ONE SONG

"GET BACK TO TOTTENHAM!"
(Chant)

Chanted at Willie Young (1977-1981) by Arsenal fans on his debut for the club, for being one of very few players to cross the North London divide. However, the crowds stance altered as he became more and more pivotal to the defence, and showed aggression and character in his robust tackling. This acceptance became cult status and led to a self explanatory and amusing double entendre song:

**"WE'VE GOT THE BIGGEST WILLIE, IN THE LAND,
WE'VE GOT THE BIGGEST WILLIE, IN THE LAND,
WE'VE GOT THE BIGGEST WILLIE, IN THE LAND,"**
(Whole World in our hands)

Young, aside from appearing in all four Cup finals reached between 1978-80, was also singlehandedly responsible for altering the rules about the professional foul. This occurred when he chopped Paul Allen down just outside the penalty area in one of the most amusing fouls seen at Wembley, and the only highlight of the 1980 FA Cup final.

His cynical transgression merely earned a free kick and a booking. The yellow card he received sent the TV studio into apoplexy, especially Jimmy Hill, and shortly afterwards the football authorities decided to alter the professional foul denying a goal scoring chance to be a red card offence.

**"SIX FOOT TWO, EYES OF BLUE,
WILLIE YOUNG IS AFTER YOU,
LA LA LA LA LA LA LA LA LA"**
(Give a Dog a Bone)

After 237 appearances he moved on to play under Brian Clough at Forest.

**"ONE LIAM BRADY,
THERE'S ONLY ONE LIAM BRADY,
ONE LIAM BRADY,
THERE'S ONLY ONE LIAM BRADY!"**
(Guantanamera)

"One Liam Brady..." after being sung lustily and heartily at Wembley was hijacked on the Morecambe and Wise show in the week after the 1979 FA cup final triumph. They used the refrain all through the programme, as Morecambe would just sing it in mid joke. Arsenal fans songs had made it mainstream at this heady time into the sketches of the most famous comedy duo on TV!

Liam Brady (1971-1980) was the idol of the North Bank in the mid to late 1970s, and for many fans a personal hero after notching 59 goals in 307 games. A gifted left footer he became an Arsenal apprentice in June 1971 and made his debut in October 1973. On his debut he came on for Jeff Blockley; surely the most

An Artist

THE ARSENAL

the possessor of a left foot that turned football into an art form... an artist amongst yeomen obvious case of beauty replaces the beast in football. His sumptuous banana shot in 1978 at Spurs, in the 5-0 win, is the most audacious and best Arsenal goal we've seen against Tottenham.

He left the club soon after the European Cup Winners Cup defeat in 1980 with the best wishes of the fans, unlike his fellow Irishman Stapleton, who left a year later to mass opprobrium. And this despite his move to Juventus being much drawn out for a ridiculously low transfer fee.

**"ALEXIS SANCHEZ BABY,
ALEXIS SANCHEZ, OH-OH-OH-OH!"**
(Don't you want me Baby - Human League)

What is it with Alexis Sanchez (2014-2018) and 1980s hits?

"WE'RE GONNA ROCK DOWN TO… ALEXIS AVENUE"
(Electric Avenue)

Chants don't always emanate from the locals. In the great Canadian city of Toronto, just on the outskirts of the city centre, there lies a Gooner pub called The Midtown Gastro Hub (Formally the Fox and Fiddle) which is run by the supporter group Arsenal Canada. The walls are decorated in Arsenal, and on a match-day will be packed full of 'T-Dot' Arsenal fans as if it were a pub in Highbury or Finsbury Park. Matt was there in 2014 during a 2-2 home draw with Hull City, when he heard the Eddy Grant chant for Sanchez.

"ALEXIS ON FIRE!"
(Your sex is on fire)

Songs for Alexis Sanchez finally come into the 21st Century.

"OH SANTI CAZORLA"
(Seven Nation Army by The White Stripes)

FA Cup final 2014; Underdog Hull City surprisingly led 2-0 from two early goals within just eight minutes of kick off. Some fans in the stands were fuming and a loss would have meant nine straight years without a trophy. Up stepped Santi to curl a free kick into the top corner and the comeback was on. From that point you just knew Arsenal would get back in the game and goals from Laurent Koscielny and Aaron Ramsey won the club a record equalling 11 FA Cups.

**"DER, DER, DER, DER, DANNY WELBECK,
DER, DER, DER, DER, DANNY WELBECK"**
(Papa's Got a Brand new Pigbag)

A modern slant on the tradition of a simple name chant for the popular Mancunian forward. He arrived at Arsenal at the end of transfer deadline day in September 2014, making his former team pay a price with the winner in the Quarter final of the FA cup at Old Trafford later that season. Sadly his prime has been blighted by injury.

**"OOH AHH, RAY PARLOUR,
I SAID OOOH AAH RAY PARLOUR"**
(Chant)

Romford's Pele first joined Arsenal in 1988. He signed on as a trainee a year later and made it to the first team in January 1992 when Arsenal were defending champions. On his debut, a midweek game at Anfield, Parlour played well but gave away a penalty which was converted in a 2-0 defeat.

It would not be until 1997 that Parlour became a regular and, under the management of George Graham, Bruce Rioch and Arsene Wenger would play 466 games and bag multiple winners' medals; most notably the 2002 FA Cup win where Parlour scored a stunning opening goal in a 2-0 win over Chelsea to secure the League and Cup double. Parlour was an 'Invincible' and left for Middlesbrough in the summer after the 2004 unbeaten title win.

Famously not picked for the England 1998 World Cup squad managed by Tottenham's Glen Hoddle after asking Hoddle's mystic for a "short back and sides", while she laid her 'healing hands' on his head.

**"VIEIRA, WOO OO OO OH, (Repeat once)
HE COMES FROM SENEGAL,
HE PLAYS FOR ARS-EN-AL!"**
(Volare – Dean Martin)

On his debut, Patrick Viera (1996-2005) was so impressive and domineering, that chants of his name rang out round Highbury. He'd come on as a substitute against Sheffield Wednesday in 1996 when Arsenal were losing 1-0. The introduction of 'Paddy' turned the game and Arsenal won 4-1. Great players deserve great chants, but rarely get them, but within a few weeks the famous Senegal song was ringing round Highbury.

Truly an Arsenal great, this 'Invincible' ran the Arsenal midfield for almost a decade and his rivalry with Roy Keane of Manchester United was the stuff of legend. He bowed out with the winning penalty in the 2005 FA cup final win after 406 appearances. In the years that followed, Arsenal never replaced his indomitable spirit, and without Vieira became prone to be being bullied and rolled over by more physical teams.

**"THERE'S ONLY ONE DENNIS BERGKAMP,
ONE DENNIS BERGKAMP,
WALKING ALONG,
SINGING A SONG,
WALKING IN A BERGKAMP WONDERLAND!"**
(Winter Wonderland)

ARSENAL

This chant is now heard everywhere and used for a number of players of all clubs – as well as seemingly every British boxer who steps into the ring.

The 'Ice Man' Bergkamp (1995-2006) got the chant before anyone else after he joined the Arsenal and would, in the eyes on many, be considered the greatest ever player in the club's history. Vying in the elite category with teammate Thierry Henry, 1970s magician Liam Brady and 1930s icon Alex James.

This 'Invincible' has a statue, commissioned by the club, after 423 appearances led to many trophies and memories of 120 great goals - including that unique Newcastle moment. However there was anoher unlikely candidate for wonderland status in 2000!

**"THERE'S ONLY ONE GRAHAM BARRETT,
ONE GRAHAM BARRETT,
WALKING ALONG,
SINGING A SONG,
WALKING IN A BARRETT WONDERLAND."**
(Winter Wonderland)

On 15 January 2000 Graham Barrett (yes that Graham Barrett) was sent on for his home debut with about five minutes to go. Barrett (1997-2003) a youth signing went onto make three appearances for the club in between loans to various sides before moving from Highbury to Coventry.

Both Matt and eminent Arsenal historian Andy Kelly were in the North Bank as this stand led the chanting for Barrett. It lasted for a couple of minutes and was to travel around the whole ground. No one appears to know why it started, or how it became infectious and why all joined in, but was one of those joyous crowd moments which all who were there will remember.

**"WE'VE GOT GEORDIE, GEORDIE ARMSTRONG ON THE WING,
ON THE WING (repeat once)
GEORDIE, GEORDIE ARMSTRONG, GEORDIE ARMSTRONG ON THE WING,
GEORDIE, GEORDIE ARMSTRONG,
GEORDIE ARMSTRONG ON THE WING."**
(Chant)

Double winner George Armstrong (1961-1977) held the record for most Arsenal appearances at 621 for the club - before David O'Leary overtook him in 1990. In the early 1970s it appeared that nearly all the Gunners' goals originated from the crossing prowess of Geordie, a genuinely effective box to box winger.

"BRIAN, BRIAN MARWOOD, BRIAN MARWOOD ON THE WING
(Chant)

A version of the Armstrong chant was reborn in the late 1980s in the Championship season of 1988-89, for Brian Marwood (1988-1990). And it was also used for Tony Adams on the rare occasions when he made a dashing run down the wing.

**"LIONEL, LIONEL RITCHIE,
LIONEL RITCHIE ON THE WING!"**

At the time, many fans believed that Glenn Helder bore a resemblance to singer Lionel Ritchie, and in his honour, they also sung this to the Marwood tune. On his Arsenal debut against Nottingham Forest in 1995 he was by far the best player on the pitch and looked truly world class. He tore the Forest defenders to shreds in what became a one man show. Arsenal fans thought we had a new super star – we were sadly wrong. If Helder had shown the same footballing talent at Arsenal that the be-permed pop master had with music – then all would have been right. But as Glenn Helder (1995-1997) was the final transfer of Graham's tenure he is also synonymous with the great manager's departure. Signed from Vitesse Arnhem he ran up and down the wing, generally fruitlessly for 49 games before moving on to Breda. But at least he got a song!

**"OVERMARS, SUPERSTAR,
WE KNOW YOU'RE BETTER THAN GINOLA!"**
(Jesus Christ Superstar)

Marc Overmars (1997-2000) was a lightening quick mercurial goal-scoring winger who in his three seasons at the club made 142 appearances and scored 41 times. In his first season Overmars scored the winner at Old Trafford to propel Arsenal onto the League, after bookies had paid out on Manchester United, so far ahead at one point were the northerners. He also scored in the FA Cup final as the Gunners completed their second double. Overmars was also the inventor of the 'Romford Pele' nickname for Ray Parlour.

In September 2016 Arsenal Legends played AC Milan Glory at the Emirates Stadium for a charity game. The general consensus was that even though he was long retired and had developed a bit of a belly, Marc Overmars was the best on the pitch and played a blinder.

**"SUPER, SUPER SWEDE, (Repeat twice)
SUPER ANDERS LIMPAR"**
(Skip To My Lou)

The original prototype for Marc Overmars was the electric fast winger Anders Limpar (1990-1994) who on his day was unplayable - pure magic, finding angles you never knew existed; but unlike Overmars, he was inconsistent and had too many off days. Limpar moved on to Everton after 116 Arsenal appearances; far too few for a player of his class. Gunners youth prodigy, Kevin Campbell; 'SUPER KEV' (1985-95), was given the same terrace chant as Limpar in the early nineties. A major contributor in George Graham's forward line up, Campbell scored 59 times in 228 games, while gaining League, FA Cup, League Cup and ECWC winners' medals at Highbury. This chant was reborn for both Robert Pires; 'SUPER ROB' (2000-2006) and Tomas Rosicky; 'SUPER TOM' (2006-2016). 'Invincible' Pires was a magician with the ball who left the club too early after 284 appearances. Rosicky never fulfilled his true potential owing to a terrible injury record only being able to play 246 times (though 88 were as substitute) in ten years at the club. Both Pires and Limpar joined Overmars for the Legends match in September 2016. The chant was also used for Jack Wilshere, being heard away at Sunderland in April 2016 as 'SUPER JACK' was greeted onto the pitch after ten months out of action.

"DON'T BLAME IT ON SUNSHINE,
DON'T BLAME IT ON MOONLIGHT,
DON'T BLAME IT ON GOOD TIMES,
BLAME IT ON EBOUE!"
(Blame it on the Boogie)

Poor Emmanuel Eboue (2005-2011) got booed by his own fans against Wigan in 2008 after a long run of below par performances. In the following couple of seasons, his heart and enthusiasm won him over with the fans - and he even got a couple of chants.

"COME TO SEE EBOUE,
YOU'VE ONLY COME TO SEE EBOUE!"
(Gauntanemera)

Well didn't we all? When Eboue left Arsenal after 214 games, 40,000 season tickets were handed back within one hour.

"HOW DOES IT FEEL TO BE TOTTENHAM?
HOW DOES IT FEEL TO BE SMALL?
YOU SOLD BALE,
WE SIGNED MESUT OZIL,
MESUT OZIL!"
(This Is How It Feels - Inspiral Carpets)

The true art form of the football chant is here in all its glory. Managing as it does to not only to sing the praises of a player, but it also gets in digs to your local rival. At the time of his signing, Mesut Ozil (2013-present) commanded Arsenal's highest ever transfer fee and after eight seasons of trophy famine - greeted his first four seasons at Arsenal with three FA Cup final wins at Wembley.

"WE'VE GOT OZIL,
MESUT OZIL,
I JUST DON'T THINK YOU UNDERSTAND,
HE'S ARSENE WENGER'S MAN,
HE'S BETTER THAN ZIDANE,
WE'VE GOT MESUT OZIL!"
(Achy Breaky Heart)

This was sung at Stoke in 2016 at halftime in the bar areas of the stadium. Flares were flying, beers swirling and fans jumping. The ultra style reaction was the in total and complete contrast to how Arsenal fans are viewed. Just shows you what happens when fans are allowed to decide for themselves who to stand with. It has become a staple, if now slightly flat, at Ashburton Grove and was the 2016/17 season anthem.

**"BIG FUCKING GERMAN,
WE'VE GOT A BIG FUCKING GERMAN."**
(Guantanamera)

Per Mertesacker (2011-2018), a triple FA Cup winner, is the BFG. This chant was a wholesale improvement to one of the most embarrassing player chants ever. Not just Arsenal, but ever. His other song "HEY MERTESACKER" was to the tune of the Euro pop classic 'Hey Margarita' and included a dance in which [a small minority of] fans would stand in a circle, wiggle and gyrate their hips. Let's move on.

"DIABY, DIABY, HE KNOCKED OUT JOHN TERRY, DIABY!"
(Let it Be)

Pretty much all he did, as he was kept on the club's wage bill far too long, but what a memory!

**"DO DO DO DO DO DO,
DO DO DO DO DO DO,
DO DO DO DO DO DO,
AARON RAMSEY!"**
(Just can't get enough)

Depeche Mode and Arsenal - What can go wrong?

**"OH ROCKY, ROCKY,
ROCKY, ROCKY, ROCKY,
ROCASTLE."**
(Son of my Father by Chicory Tip)

"Hi Tim, sorry about the delay in replying to your letter. It's great to know that I've got support like you cheering me and the team on. I hope you enjoyed the win over Spurs, and hopefully we'll win something this year. Best wishes, David Rocastle." Letter to Arsenal fan Tim Howorth from David in 1987. Tim had sent Rocastle a letter thanking him and the team for beating Spurs in the 1987 League Cup semi-final.

That letter sums up David Rocastle (1983-1992) who died of throat cancer in 2001. Everyone loved him. Everyone respected him as a wonderful human being and as one of the greatest midfielders in Arsenal history. In each of his 277 appearances he juggled grace with steel, as while a fantastic ball player - he could also look after himself on the pitch.

On 31 March 2001 Arsenal hosted a league game against local rivals Tottenham Hotspur. In the Gunners Pub before the game, fans were chanting the name of this legend who hadn't played for the club for nearly ten years. 'OH ROCKY ROCKY… ROCKY ROCKY ROCKY ROCKY ROCASTLE!'

Matt recalls thinking that's good to hear, but why now? Why are they singing the name of Rocastle today? Deep in the back of my mind I had some trepidation about the chant, because I was aware that David Rocastle was fighting a battle with cancer.

Inside Highbury, the kick off was imminent and then alarmingly, Rocastle's face appeared on the two big TV screens in the two corners of the stadium. Many of us had no idea that he had passed away and this was the first we heard of what happened. This was more than sad news, this was an absolute tragedy and all hopes of the following 90 minutes suddenly became insignificant.

The stadium announcer confirmed that Rocastle had lost his fight with illness and for everyone present to hold a minute's silence. The silence that followed gets talked about on a regular basis when remembering Rocky - and the common point of discussion was the respectful and classy way that Spurs fans observed it. Sometimes silence is very welcome and sometimes we can all stand together in respect.

Every year on the home game nearest his tragic passing 'OH ROCKY ROCKY… ROCKY ROCKY ROCKY ROCKY ROCASTLE' is heard from the stands commemorating a true Gunner legend.

"SEAMAN,
DO THE TWIST,
SEAMAN, SEAMAN,
DO THE TWIST"

David Seaman (1990-2003), smiling but looking embarrassed, had no choice but to move his feet whenever the North Bank or Clock End lost interest in the game and turned their attention elsewhere, demanding he perform for them. After replacing the popular John Lukic he played 564 times and was a rock behind the legendary back four.

He put his twisting training to great use, when in the 2003 Semi Final, he pulled off a wonder save late in the game to keep the score at 1-0, and ensure Arsenal went onto Cardiff. Of all the great saves he made in his career, that was generally considered the most memorable. Also the single name chant for "SEAMAN" morphed easily into his replacement between the sticks: "LEHMAN"

"HE'S BLONDE,
HE'S QUICK,
HIS NAME'S A PORNO FLICK,
EMMANUEL, EMMANUEL!"
(In the Quarter Master's Store)

Not much to say aside from Emmanuel Petit's (1997-2000) song is one of the wittiest player chants of all time. Petit was a great foil alongside countryman Vieira in his three seasons at the club while amassing 118 games and was a double winner in 1997/98.

**"HE'S QUICK, HE'S BLONDE,
HE WON THE COUPE DU MONDE,
EMMANUEL, EMMANUEL!"**
(In the Quarter Master's Store)

In the dying seconds of the 1998 World Cup Final, France were 2-0 up and substitute Patrick Vieira dribbled towards the Brazil goal. He played a through pass to Petit who placed the ball in the bottom corner to make it 3-0 and seal France's first ever World Cup Win. The next day the Daily Mirror proclaimed that Arsenal had won the World Cup!

**"HE'S BIG,
HE'S BLACK,
HE'S HAD A HEART ATTACK,
KING KANU, KING KANU!"**
(In the Quarter Master's Store)

The Daily Mirror nominated this as one of the worst chants of the season, no doubt because some people might consider it in poor taste; and of course if there's one thing tabloid newspapers always do - is conduct themselves with the highest of standards in every way. God forbid that poor taste ever found its way into the newspapers.

In 1996 Nwankwo Kanu (1999-2004) was a star of the Nigerian Olympic gold medal team that beat Brazil in the final, and later that year Kanu was diagnosed with a heart default and had to undergo surgery to remove a valve. So he never actually had a heart attack – but please don't let facts get in the way of a good sing song. Kanu went on to set up a heart foundation in Africa for children with heart diseases. All hail the King. A highly popular player, he appeared 198 times for the Gunners which included the 'Invincible' season. He came back for one last game in 2016 when Arsenal Legends beat AC Milan Glory – and Kanu scored a hat trick.

**"CHIM-CHIMNEY, CHIM-CHIMNEY,
CHIM-CHIM-CHEROO,
WHO NEEDS ANELKA?
WHEN WE'VE GOT KANU!"**
(Chim Chimney from Mary Poppins)

Nicolas Anelka (1997-99) had been a striking partner with Kanu in the 1998-99 season but left in the summer to join Real Madrid, ensuring a huge profit for the club. Despite a fine goal scoring record Anelka never truly won the hearts of the fans - unlike Kanu who was an instant favourite.

"HE'S 5 FOOT 4,
HE'S 5 FOOT 4,
WE'VE GOT ARSHAVIN,
FUCK ADEBAYOR!"
(Sloop John B)

Unfortunately the initial and fully justified excitement over the acquisition of Arshavin dribbled away, as he was persistently played out of position.

"WHOOPSY DAISY,
MARTIN HAYESY,
LA, LA, LA-LA-LA, LA!"
(Cock O' The North)

Martin Hayes (1982-1990) was an apprentice who worked his way through the ranks and scored 34 goals in his 132 games for Arsenal. The majority of these came during his second season in 1986/87 when he was the club's top scorer with 24 goals, half of which were from the penalty spot. He never made it to fan favourite status, but was a cult hero to many, and his song does have a bumbling tone to it. A skilful player he never had the confidence to push himself forward to fully realise his ability.

Arsenal though would never have won the league title in 1988/89 had it not been for Hayes. At the tail end of the season he scored the only goal in a 1-0 win at Middlesbrough which would go on to prove decisive. As a second half substitute at Anfield in 1989, he was on the field when Michael Thomas scored; making him one of only 13 players who played in the most famous single game in the club's history.

"WE ALL AGREE,
RIXY IS BETTER THAN HODDLE!"
(Cielito Lindo, AKA the Ay, Ay, Ay, Ay song)

Graham Rix (1974-1988) taken on by Arsenal as an apprentice, made his debut in April 1977 and soon after became a first team regular who made 464 appearances. Rix provided the cross for the last minute Alan Sunderland FA Cup final goal in 1979, and his silky skills made him a crowd favourite. As an England International, Rix was a genuine competitor to the golden boy Hoddle.

But in 1999, a long time after he had left, his relationship with Arsenal fans did turn sourer after he was convicted of having sex with an underage girl. After release from prison, Rix returned to Chelsea as part of the coaching staff where he had been since 1995.

Sections of the Arsenal support would chant songs about Rix, which included a song about his girlfriend only being four years old (the girl related to his conviction was 15 years of age at the time of the offence).

Rix returned to Arsenal as a guest of honour in 2006 for the last ever game at Highbury and got a polite reception as opposed to good or bad one.

WE'VE ONLY GOT ONE SONG

"AT NUMBER 1, IT'S PERRY GROVES,
AT NUMBER 2, IT'S PERRY GROVES,
AT NUMBER 3, IT'S PERRY GROVES,
AT NUMBER 4, IT'S PERRY GROVES,
AT NUMBER 5, IT'S PERRY GROVES,
AT NUMBER 6, IT'S PERRY GROVES,
AT NUMBER 7, IT'S PERRY GROVES,
AT NUMBER 8, IT'S PERRY GROVES,
AT NUMBER 9, IT'S PERRY GROVES,
AT NUMBER 10, IT'S PERRY GROVES,
AT NUMBER 11, IT'S PERRY GROVES,
AT NUMBER 12, IT'S PERRY GROVES,
WE ALL LIVE IN A PERRY GROVES WORLD,
A PERRY GROVES WORLD,
A PERRY GROVES WORLD!" (repeat)
(Yellow submarine by the Beatles)

A different version had Liam Brady at no 7, when fans got bored of singing Perry Groves. However, no other player was allowed to inhabit Perry's world in a song which was popularised around the time of the 1991 Championship win.

Perry Groves (1986-1992) was George Graham's first purchase. Coming from Colchester he went onto appear 203 times for the Gunners.

Quick and hard-working, he was a fan favourite and even more so after clobbering Graham Roberts with a naughty tackle at Stamford Bridge in September 1989, which saw the ex-Spurs man taken off on a stretcher. Roberts was one of the most despised opposition players among the Arsenal 1980s support. The season prior, like Martin Hayes, Groves was on the field when Michael Thomas scored at Anfield.

"WE LOVE YOU FREDDIE,
COS YOU'VE GOT RED HAIR,
WE LOVE YOU FREDDIE,
COS YOU'RE EVERYWHERE,
WE LOVE YOU FREDDIE,
COS YOU'RE ARSENAL THROUGH AND THROUGH!"
(Can't Take My Eyes Off You (I Love You Baby)
the Andy Williams version)

"WE LOVE YOU FREDDIE,
COS YOU'VE GOT NO HAIR,
WE LOVE YOU FREDDIE,
COS YOU'RE EVERYWHERE,
WE LOVE YOU FREDDIE,
COS YOU'RE ARSENAL THROUGH AND THROUGH!"
(Can't Take My Eyes Off You (I Love You Baby)
the Andy Williams version)

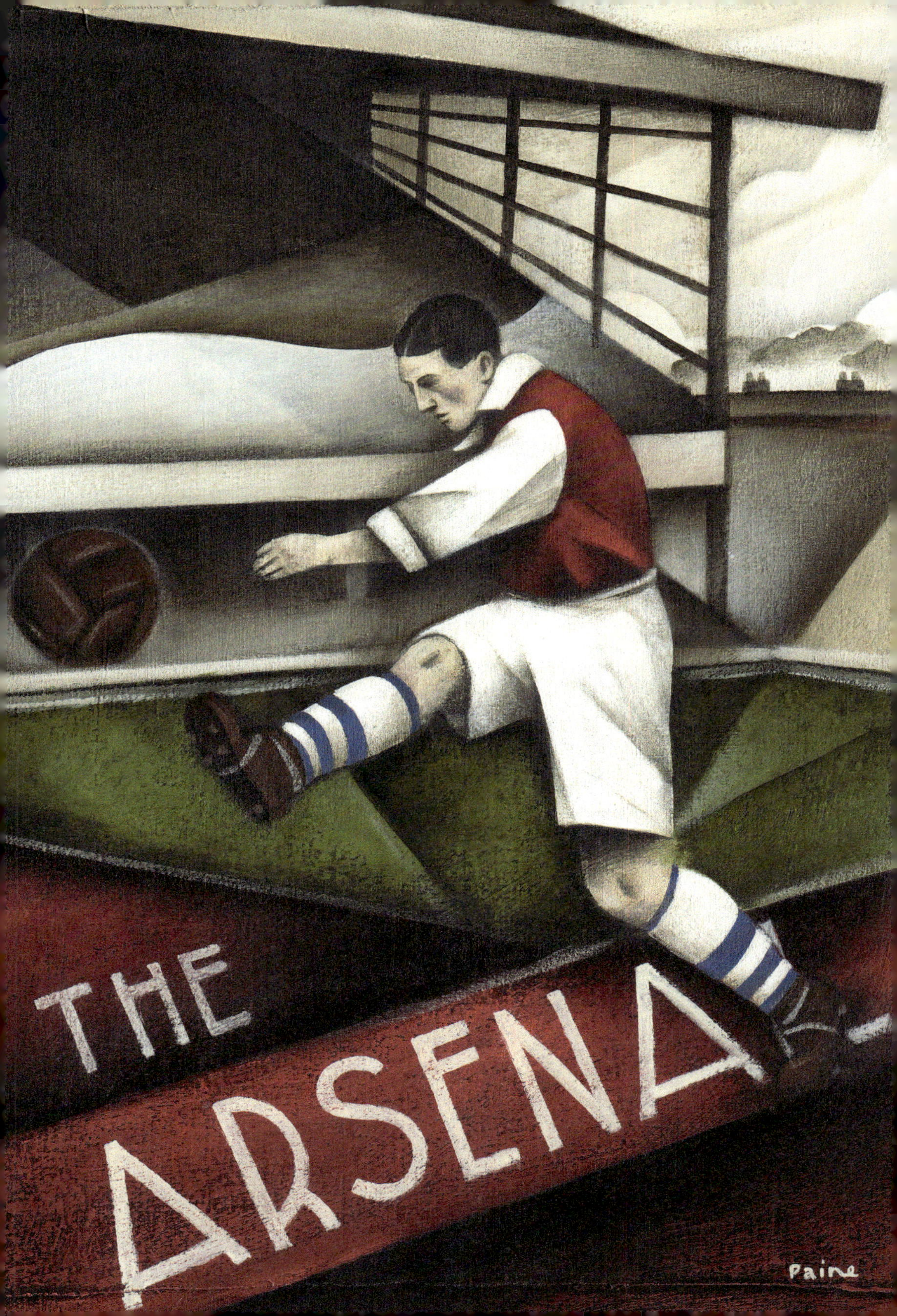
THE
ARSENA
Paine

WE'VE ONLY GOT ONE SONG

Two basic versions were sung dependent on the barnet sported by Freddie Ljungberg (1998-2007). The red hair version being particular to the 2001-02 season, and is the song we think of when remembering that double season, especially as he did not appear to be able to stop scoring in the final few games; the Swede truly was the driving force in the tail end of the double season. A massively popular 'Invincible' his 328 games were too few for his talent, but injuries marred his career at Arsenal.

> "NANANANANANANANANANANA,
> HECTOR BELLERIN, BELLERIN,
> HECTOR BELLERIN!"

(Baby give it up - KC and the Sunshine band)

Heard as he notched the third against Watford in April 2016

> "OSPINA"

(Chant)

Chanted in the format of "YOU'RE SHIT AHHHHHHHHH", which is a traditional chant for the opposition keeper while he is taking a goal kick in an attempt to put him off. But this chant is praising the Arsenal keeper David Ospina (2014-19)

> "ARSENE WENGER WENT TO BRAZIL,
> AFTER A BLOKE WITH A LOAD OF SKILL,
> AN AGENT SAID I'VE GOT THE PLAYER FOR YOU,
> HE AINT GOT A PASSPORT AND HIS NAME IS EDU,
> EDU, EDU"

(Tom Hark by the Piranhas)

After passport and Visa problems Edu Gasper finally became an Arsenal player in 2001. He made 127 appearances and scored 15 goals including a penalty in his final ever game at Highbury during a 7-0 thumping of Everton in May 2005; a match in which Arsenal wore red with white sleeves at Highbury for the last time.

> "FLAMINI, FLAMINI,
> DA DA DA DA – DA DA DA"

(Theme from the Sweeney)

A song marrying the modern player Mathieu Flamini (2004-2008 and 2013-2016) with a classic 1970s TV show; why – nobody knows other than 'Flamini' rhymes with 'The Sweeney'. After his second period with the club and 246 appearances, it would be safe to say that fans blew hot and cold with the Frenchman during his return. Though, after his wonder goal against Spurs which completed his brace in the League cup tie of 2015/16 he was back in the good books - for a while. Also an owner of a biochemical company, Flamini should have no worries after he retires from playing.

**"HE SCORES WHEN HE WANTS, (Repeat once)
ROBIN VAN PERSIE,
HE SCORES WHEN HE WANTS"**
(Sloop John B)

The immediate reaction from both authors is to snub this song. But the second more rational reaction is – no, RVP is one of only a handful of modern players who have scored over 100 goals for the club. And what goals they were; at the time they gave joy to Arsenal fans.

His move to Manchester United did dismay us all - but does that fully eclipse the memories of a raft of great goals?

Van Persie (2004-12) scored 132 goals for Arsenal and was club captain before he jumped ship to Manchester United, where he was top goal scorer in their 2012-13 title winning team. In the following years, injuries, which so dogged his Arsenal career came back to haunt him, and were seen by many as karma.

"ADEBAYOR MY LORD, ADEBAYOR"
(Kumbayar My Lord)

Similarly we would like to forget this one!

"NA-NA-NA-NA, GIROUD!"
(Hey Jude)

A great chant for Olivier Giroud (2012-2018), and within his pretty impressive 105 goals in 253 games were some stunners. None more so than the Scorpion Kick against Palace on New Year's Day 2017. This amazing effort won him the FIFA Puskas Award for goal of the year in 2017, an award for the most aesthetically pleasing strike that covers the whole world of football. What an absolute belter, best goal seen at the Emirates?

**"JOSE ANTONIO,
JOSE ANTONIO,
JOSE ANTONIO,
JOSE ANTONIO!"**
(La Donna e Mobile – Verdi)

Jose Antonio Reyes (2004-2007) came to Arsenal from Sevilla and by the end of his first season had become an 'Invincible'. He also won an FA Cup winners medal, in the process becoming only the second player to be sent off in an FA Cup final in 2005 as the Gunners beat Manchester United on penalties. After 23 goals in 110 appearances he was loaned out to Real Madrid and then moved next season to Athletico Madrid. As this book was about to be published the terribly sad news of his death at the age of 35 in a car crash was announced - RIP Jose Antonio Reyes, the 'Invincible'.

"WE WERE THERE WHEN JENSEN SCORED"
(Guide Me, O Thou Great Jehovah)

In the summer of 1992, after scoring a stunning goal in Denmark's 2-0 win against Germany in the European Championship Final – John Jensen signed for Arsenal as a replacement for David Rocastle. Hardly like for like; compared to the skill and endeavour of Rocky, Jensen was a workhorse and the goal against Germany would be the last time he hit the net until the dawn of 1995.

The 1994/95 season had been truly dismal with a committed but lacklustre midfield. George Graham was losing his magic touch, and available match tickets were easy to come by as the team slid into the bottom half of the table.

A bit like the fear of not buying a lottery ticket with the same numbers, the only reason people kept on coming to Highbury was to one day see John Jensen score a goal; that was Matt's main motivation – and yet the one home game he missed that season was the one against QPR when Jensen scored a cracker from just outside the box. Matt's fateful words before being forced to visit relatives: "I just hope Jensen doesn't score" Oh dear!

"GIVE IT TO SANCHEZ (clap clap clap clap clap)"
(Chant)

Heard at Sutton in February 2017, bringing alive reminiscences of the late 70s chants "GIVE IT TO BRADY" as the crowd demanded the ball go to the most skilful and creative payer in the team.

"PAUL MERSON, PAUL MERSON, PAUL MERSON"
(Stars and Stripes Forever)

Not really a dynamic chant, but certainly a dynamic footballer. On his day, 'the Merse' (1986-1997) was a world class attacking midfielder who scored 99 goals in 425 appearances. So close to being in the 100 club, and that one more goal - and more - surely would have come about had he not been bedevilled so many personal demons most notably drink, drugs and gambling.

By 2019 Merson was still dealing with serious gambling issues and in the ITV program 'Harry's Hero's' broke down in tears, saying how hard he was finding life. Perhaps he will always have gambling addiction, however he will also always be an Arsenal legend, winning two league titles, one FA Cup, one Cup Winners Cup and two League Cups (the second of which came in 1993 against Sheffield Wednesday when Merson scored the levelling goal on the way to a two one victory).

"ANDY LINIGHAN, ANDY LINIGHAN"
(Chirpy Chirpy Cheep Cheep)

Reliable centre back Linighan (1990-97) a George Graham signing from Norwich never quite excelled to the heights of the other Arsenal defenders of the same era, however the fan base will always fondly remember him for the winning goal in the last seconds of the 1993 FA Cup Final. The most important one of the total of eight he scored in 156 games

Matt was in the Highbury pub The Kings Head after the final game of the season in 2016 when St. Totteringham's Day was confirmed. Linighan was at the bar and happily chatting to fans. Tipsy after a few Guinness too many, he kept on pointing to his forehead, proud of the goal that won Arsenal the cup.

**"KOLO TOURE OH, OH, (Repeat once)
FROM THE COAST OF THE IVORY,
HE CAME TO HIGHBURY "**
(Volare - Dean Martin)

Toure also got a version of the Viera chant.

OPPOSITION PLAYERS

"GEORGIE BEST!
SUPERSTAR!
WALKS LIKE A WOMAN,
AND HE WEARS A BRA!"
(Jesus Christ Superstar)

Sung whenever Arsenal played Manchester United in the early 1970s. Another variant on the same theme was "GEORGIE BEST SUPERSTAR WEARS FRILLY KNICKERS AND A SEE THROUGH BRA".

However, it was also turned on our very own Charlie George, who according to Mancunians and indeed many other opposition fans - chanted allegations that: "CHARLIE GEORGE SUPERSTAR WALKS LIKE A WOMAN AND HE WEARS A BRA"

In fact any long haired flair player in any team; most notably Tony Currie, Stan Bowles or Rodney Marsh; was subject to the same good natured censure from the terraces up and down the country in the 1970s.

"TONY ADAMS' MAGIC,
HE'S GOT A MAGIC KNOB,
AND WHEN HE SAW CAPRICE,
HE STUCK IT IN HER GOB,
HE STUCK IT UP HER FANNY,
HE STUCK IT UP HER BUM,
AND WHEN HE WENT DOWN SHITE HART LANE,
HE FUCKED GLENN HODDLE'S MUM!"
(My Old Man's a Dustman)

This one-club-man, during the latter stages of his career, in around 1999, started dating model Caprice, and was greeted with this chant.

With all that 'alleged exertion' it is a wonder that he managed to fit in 669 games, the second most in club history behind David O'Leary.

"ROBSON, ROBSON MAN OF THE MATCH"

Brian Robson or 'Captain Marvel' as the media styled him was England and Manchester United's Captain in the 1980s. This is a sarcastic comment from the bowels of the North Bank on the overly fulsome praise perpetually heaped upon him, as Robson was always named man of the match however he played.

"WHAT A WASTE OF MONEY!"

Aimed at opposition players deemed not to be any good. Or just a player who cost a lot of money to buy. Rarely heard in the recent past as football has lost its bearings over the value of money.

**"ARSENAL REJECT, (Repeat once)
HELLO, HELLO"**
(Chant)

A 1980s and 1990s chant, sung to ex Arsenal players whenever they returned to Highbury, denoting that whoever they were playing for now was not at the level of 'The Arsenal'. A song contradicting the saying coined by Bob Wilson, that 'Once an Arsenal man, always an Arsenal man'.

The reject label was also handy when opponents had an ex-Spurs player in their ranks. "TOTTENHAM REJECT HELLO HELLO" amongst many other vitriolic chants would be aimed at the former Cockerel.

"MCAVENNIE IS A WANKER, IS A WANKER!"(Repeat as necessary)
(Hallelujah)

1980s playboy striker Frank McAvennie was regarded as a popular figure among Hammers fans. However, he was also regarded as a wanker by the North Bank.

"SHEARER'S A WANKER [clap, clap, clap]
(Chant - repeat as necessary)

You don't have to be witty to be funny. Arsenal v Newcastle in 1997; a boring game was lit up by the clearest, loudest, most well timed rendition of Clock End analysis on Alan Shearer.

"IT AIN'T FUCKING SHEARER"
(Chant)

That embarrassing moment when you wrongly think someone is waving at you and you wave back. Arsenal fans had been singing "THERE'S ONLY ONE ENGLAND CAPTAIN" in support of Tony Adams and Shearer applauded the Clock End to be met with the above terse response.

**"RUUD VAN SHIT HIMSELF,
TRA-LA-LA-LA-LA"**
(Brown Girl in the Ring)

At Old Trafford in 2003, Arsenal players, with Martin Keown to the fore, surrounded, pushed and mocked Ruud Van Nistelrooy for missing a late penalty. Minutes earlier Nistelrooy had managed to get Patrick Viera sent off; then to add insult to injury Forlan went down easily to win a soft penalty in injury time. In football the margins are small - one accurate penalty and the Arsenal team of 2003/04 would not be referred to as the 'Invincibles'.

**"ONE MINUTE,
ONE MINUTE,
ONE MINUTE"**
(Stars and Stripes Forever)

Anfield 89: Without question, the greatest single match in the history of Arsenal. A minute before Michael Thomas broke Scouse hearts, a finger waving Steve McMahon was highly animated in letting his teammates know how long there was left on the clock. In the following years, Arsenal fans would never let McMahon forget how long there was left, or the futility of his on pitch gesticulation.

"YOU'LL NEVER PLAY FOR ARSENAL"
(Chant)

And we were wrong. Arsenal v Aston Villa in April 1991 and George Graham's men were closing in on the league title by leading Aston Villa 4-0 at Highbury. Villa goalkeeper Nigel Spink went down injured and had to be taken off; and these were the days before goalkeepers made up the two places allocated to the options on the subs bench.

Therefore this meant that an outfield player had to go in goal and David Platt was the one to wear the goalkeeper jersey – the Arsenal goalkeeper jersey. Villa didn't have a spare one! Platt was mocked by the North Bank and looked as at home in goal as Sylvester Stallone did in 'Escape to Victory'. Kevin Campbell put one past Platt and the game ended 5-0. Boring, boring, Arsenal.

**"HE SHOT, HE MISSSED,
HE MUST BE FUCKING PISSED,
GORDON HILL,
GORDON HILL"**
(In the Quarter Master's Store)

As the Derby winger Gordon Hill ballooned yet another wayward shot over Pat Jennings' bar the terraced crowd chanted this ditty aimed at goading him and his profligacy. Many other players whose shooting appeared to carried out while wearing Toblerone shaped boots were subjected to this chant over the years, but on this cold pre-Xmas afternoon in 1978 Hill, an ex-Manchester United player, took the brunt from the North Bank.

**"OH TEDDY TEDDY,
HE WENT TO MAN UNITED,
AND HE WON FUCK ALL!"**
(Son of my Father)

Sung in 1998 after winning the title, but the following year Sheringham won the triple with Man United. In the charity Shield in August 1999 (Arsenal finishing in second played, as United won both the league and the FA cup) Sheringham warmed up in front of the Arsenal fans and held out three fingers. Therefore the song either had to be modified or dropped forever:

**"OH TEDDY, TEDDY,
YOU MIGHT HAVE WON SOME MEDALS,
BUT YOU'RE STILL A C**T!"**
(Son of my Father)

Not since Graham Roberts, had a player been so disliked by Arsenal supporters. There was something about Sheringham that just riled Arsenal fans more than anyone else. It was as if he were a human embodiment of Tottenham Hotspur (except for the medals). Matt once put a thread out on an Arsenal internet fan forum asking 'Is there a player you hate more than Sheringham?' in which the definitive response from most people was - No.

**"OH, TEDDY, TEDDY,
TEDDY, TEDDY, TEDDY, TEDDY, SHERINGHAM"**
(Son of My Father)

After the Charity Shield game in 1999, Arsenal fans outside Wembley, did indeed, sing this song without any additional words and alterations. Yes, this was the traditional song of support for Teddy Sheringham sung by Gooners – whilst circling around and pointing at a huge heap of horse manure.

**"YOU FAT BASTARD!
YOU FAT BASTARD!"**

Most notably sung at Paul Gascoigne when he joined Spurs in 1988. In the North London derby of that year, Arsenal fans littered the pitch at White Hart Lane with hundreds of mars bars aimed at Gazza. Instead of being offended, Gascoigne responded by picking up one of the Mars Bars and eating it; much to the appreciation and respect of the away end.

**"LEE BUMS BELL, BELL BUMS LEE,
BELL AND LEE BUM SUMMERBEE,
WITH A NICK-NAK-PADDY-WACK,
GIVE A DOG A BONE,
WHY DON'T CITY FUCK OFF HOME?"**
(This Old Man)

While heard around Highbury whenever City were visiting, it was also sung all over the country as Manchester City were a top team around the late 1960s and early 1970s under ex-Arsenal captain Joe Mercer's and Malcolm Allison's leadership.

All three players involved in this imaginary and tasteless menage-a-trois were England internationals, and as such targeted as they were high quality attacking players. It also helped that their surnames scanned!

**"WORSE THAN YOUR BROTHER,
YOU'RE EVEN WORSE THAN YOUR BROTHER!"**
(Guantanemera)

Sung to Phil Neville, who most likely joined in with this unarguable chant.

**"PHIL NEVILLE AND HIS BROTHER,
THEY LIKE TO SHAG THEIR MOTHER,
THEY ALL SHAG EACH OTHER,
THE NEVILLE FAMILY!"**
(The Adam's Family)

Though we're sure Phil preferred the first song to this one, an example that fans will stoop to appalling levels to try to get under the skin of opponents.

**"COCKERILL, HOW'S YOUR JAW?
COCKERILL, COCKERILL, HOW'S YOUR JAW?"**
(Chant)

In 1988 Paul Davis knocked out Glenn Cockerill on the centre circle at Highbury with a brutal upper cut. It wasn't spotted by the match day officials and Cockerill's jaw was broken in two places. The FA would go on to fine Davis £3,000 (a big chunk of cheese in 1988) and give him a nine match ban.

Sympathy for Cockerill was lacking from the Highbury crowd, as preceding the upper cut, Cockerill had been dishing out abuse to Davis throughout the whole game. Instead of condemnation, Davis got a new chant and song.

"TYSON RUNS FROM DAVIS, LA LA LA LA LA LA LA LA"
(Let's All Do The Conga)

**"WE ALL AGREE,
DAVIS IS BETTER THAN TYSON!"**
(Cielito Lindo, AKA the Ay, Ay, Ay, Ay song)

Paul Davis (1977-1995) signed as an apprentice in 1977, made his debut in 1980 and was a fixture in the team by the 1981/82 season. He made 447 appearances in the red and white, having a hand in all the trophies Arsenal won under George Graham. Though just after this incident there was a period where Graham hardly used him for close to two years until the start of the

1990/91 season; maybe suggesting some sort of a rift between the two. In 1989 Mike Tyson was the heavyweight champion of the world - undefeated and pummelling the division dry of contenders.

"LET HIM DIE!" (Repeat multiple times)
(Stars and Stripes Forever)

Not heard anymore, but always a regular in the Highbury years during the 1980s and 1990s whenever an opposition player was on the floor and needed treatment.

"BRING ON THE DUSTBIN!"
(Branston Pickle advert)

A less brutal version of the song above!

**"FUCK OFF PINOCCHIO,
FUCK OFF PINOCCHIO!"**
(La Donna e Mobile - Verdi)

Traditional greeting towards Phil Thompson the large nosed defender and later coach of Liverpool, now a Sky pundit with our own Charlie Nicholas.

"TINA, TINA, TINA"
(chant)

**"SHILTON HIT A LAMP POST,
SHILTON HIT A LAMP POST,
LALALALA, LALALALA"**
(Let's all do the Conga)

"DOES YOUR MISSES KNOW YOU'RE HERE?"
(Guide me O, Thou Great Jehovah)

"THERE WAS NO HANKY PANKY"
(Guantanamera)

According to contemporary newspaper reports, early on a May morning in 1980, the England goalkeeper, Peter Shilton's car windows were steamed up in a secluded Nottingham lane with a married woman called Tina Street inside his Daimler. Tina's husband Colin arrived with the pair partially clothed, leading to Shilton hurriedly driving away to avoid the angry husband. Unfortunately for Shilton, he crashed into a lamp post and was arrested for drink-driving as the police had just arrived on the scene. He was fined £350 and banned from driving for 15 months.

His torment did not end there, as after the front page reports of the "England goalie and the girl who went to extra time" had appeared in the Mirror he had to endure countless terrace chants for much of the rest of his career.

The reports of his being caught with Tina - appeared just prior to Arsenal versus Forest on 27 September 1980 at Highbury. So amusingly the North Bank, the Clock End, and the East and West stands got first go at the chants!

When he arrived at the ground he was met with rousing cries of "Tina, Tina, Tina" which reportedly tickled Brian Clough, Peter Taylor and all his team mates as they entered via the marble halls.

The same refrain continually went around all parts of the ground, and the North Bank chant "There was no hanky panky" a reference to an Express headline even brought a smile from Shilton himself. Other good natured and more ribald chants such as "HE SHOT, HE CUM, ALL OVER TINA'S BUM, SHILTON, SHILTON" were heard and for almost the full 90 minutes as the crowd effectively ignored the match and indulged themselves in fun at the expense of England's premier goalie and philanderer.

To make matters worse for him, the Gunners won 1-0 after a mistake by Shilton, who for whatever reason, may have had other things on his mind.

This incident was quite ironic as two years earlier "Tina and the North Bank" had released a record called "Come on You Gunners" in May 1978. It was of course just a coincidence and was not the same Tina who took Shilton to extra time. Tina's song is below.

"TO WEAR RED AND WHITE, GIVES COURAGE TO FIGHT,
AND NEVER SAY DIE TIL THE END.
"TO SEE RED AND WHITE, IT'S OUR HEART'S DELIGHT,
SO PROUD THAT WE'LL SING IT AGAIN…
COME ON YOU GUNNERS, COME ON YOU GUNNERS
SHOW THE WORLD WHAT YOU CAN DO
COME ON YOU GUNNERS, COME ON YOU GUNNERS
GIVE US A GOAL BOYS,
A GLORIOUS GOAL, BOYS.
GIVE US ANOTHER ONE, TOO-OOOOO."

Wonder why it didn't catch on…?

"SHILTON BEATS HIS WIFE UP,
SHILTON BEATS HIS WIFE UP,
LA LA LA LA,
LA LA LA LA!"
(Let's all do the Conga)

Almost a decade later Shilton, then at Derby, came to Highbury in May 1989 as the Rams beat Arsenal at home and looked like scuppering the team's chances for the title. Shilton, who played a blinder, responded to the cruel and unfounded chant with a Charlie George style V sign.

"SQUIRREL, SQUIRREL, SQUIRREL"
(Chant)

MIDDLESBROUGH'S DAVID ARMSTRONG HANDS OFF LIAM BRADY

Not so much an opposition player, but who can forget the little intruder who invaded the Highbury pitch in 2006 when Arsenal played a Champions League semi-final against Villarreal. The squirrel even got a chant and many joked, sorry, - stated the undeniable fact, - that the squirrel had more Champions league appearances than Tottenham at the time.

"YOU'RE SO FAT IT'S UNBELIEVABLE!"
(Chant)

To Hans Segers, Neil Webb and Jan Molby to name but a few slightly portly opponents

"SKINHEAD, SKINHEAD"
(Chant)

To David Armstrong of Boro and Saints who at a very young age was almost totally bald.

**"MABBUTT IS A JUNKIE,
LALALALALALA"**
(Let's All Do the Conga)

To Gary Mabbutt after it was revealed he was diabetic and had to inject himself.

**"GARY MABBUT, GARY MABBUT,
WHAT'S IT LIKE TO HAVE NO SWEETS"**
(Guide me, O Thou Great Jehovah)

Spurs captain Gary Mabbutt battled diabetes during his entire career.

"YOU'RE JUST A GREEDY C*NT, STAPLETON, STAPLETON"
(We'll take more care of you - BT advert)

Frank Stapleton (1972-1981) was signed in the summer of 1972 as an apprentice. He progressed through the ranks and was a regular first team player from 1976-77 onwards. He scored 108 goals for the club including a first half goal against Manchester United in the legendary FA Cup "five minute" final of 1979.

When he signed for Manchester United in 1981 the Highbury crowd, many of whom had seen him play for youth and reserves team saw this as a gross betrayal by "one of our own". They were unforgiving and accused him via the above chant, and other more robust means, of only leaving for the money. While at Man Utd he won two FA Cup winners medals. In the same period Arsenal won the League Cup once.

"OH WANKY WANKY, WANKY WANKY WANKY WANKY, STAPLETON"
(Son of My Father)

This was also sung frequently after Frank Stapleton left us in 1981 and played for Manchester United. Previously one of his occasional songs had been:

"OH FRANKY FRANKY, FRANKY, FRANKY, FRANKY, FRANKY, STAPLETON"
(Son of My Father)

Before his defection he was popular but afterwards he was reviled. Two decades later and little changes:

"OH ASHLEY COLE, HE'S A FUCKING ARSEHOLE" (Repeat multiple times)
(Cielito Lindo, AKA the Ay, Ay, Ay, Ay song)

Ashley Cole (1997-2006) a product of the Arsenal youth system from 1997, progressed through the ranks; becoming a regular from 2001 onwards. He was one of the 'Invincibles' winning three FA Cup medals and two Premier League winners medals while at Highbury.

But he left for Chelsea in 2006 because he reportedly felt 'physically sick' when offered "only" £55,000 a week while the Blues were offering an alleged £90K per week: cue Frank Stapleton saying 'and they called me greedy!'

In fairness to Cole, his move would bring him many trophies as well as money. He helped Chelsea win the Champions, Europa and Premier Leagues and four FA Cups. Consequently he holds the individual record for most FA Cup winners' medals at seven. During the same period, Arsenal won nothing.

**"OH WANKY WANKY,
WANKY WANKY WANKY WANKY, WORTHINGTON"**
(Son of My Father)

Sung for ladies man, and geninely talented forward, Frank Worthington, who seemed to go through many teams, though never sung with as much gusto as for Stapleton.

**"SAMI YOU'RE A C*NT
YOU'RE A C*NT
SAMI YOU'RE A C*NT"**
(Baby Give it Up)

Once again, an Arsenal player moved on, claiming he wanted to win trophies, whilst many fans shared a different view and accused him of only being money motivated. Samir Nasri (2008-11) had played 125 matches for the club before leaving. His best football for Arsenal was in 2010/11 and off the back of that - he became in demand most notably from oil rich Manchester City. During this time, many fans also turned their attention on the Arsenal board and accused the club of being all too happy to sell off the best players. This song was to the same tune as Nasri's chant when he was an Arsenal player – but with C*nt replacing Nasri.

"84... SHE'S 84, WAYNE ROONEY'S GIRLFRIEND IS 84"
(Tom Hark by the Piranhas)

Sung around the time of a scurrilous tabloid 'exclusive'!

**"BARNESY, BARNESY WHAT'S THE SCORE?"
BARNESY WHAT'S THE SCORE?**
(Chant)

In the days before digital scoreboards, fans and players sometimes needed to be reminded what the score was. This was sung to John Barnes as Anders Limpar ran rings around Liverpool at Highbury in April 1992. The 4-0 score line was a poor reflection of Arsenal's dominance on that day, where both authors saw that Limpar long distance wonder goal.

**"WHO'S UP MARY BROWN? WHO'S UP MARY BROWN?
TOMMY TOMMY DOCHERTY,
TOMMY TOMMY DOCHERTY!"**
(Knees up Mother Brown)

Manchester United manager Tommy Docherty, and ex Arsenal player (1958-1961) was caught having an affair with the physio's wife Mary Brown in the late 1970s.

WE'VE ONLY GOT ONE SONG

"ARDILES IS A WANKER,
HE COMES FROM ARGENTINA,
AND VILLA IS A POOFTA,
WHO SUCKS OSSIE'S COCK!"
(Messing about on the River)

The double signings of Ossie Ardiles and Ricky Villa for Spurs in the early 1980s was during an era when Britain was at war with Argentina and an era before anybody would have had their complaint about homophobic chanting in football listened to.

"YOU THOUGHT YOU HAD SCORED,
YOU WERE WRONG, YOU WERE WRONG"
(We'll take more care of you - BT advert)

Sung to an opposition player, or set of opposing fans, generally when a shot goes into the side netting and they believe a goal has been scored. But it hasn't. Comes with optional desultory hand gestures!

"ROY KEANE WO-OH, (Repeat Once)
FOR 50,000 QUID,
HE SCORED FOR REAL MADRID!"
(Volare - Dean Martin)

In the year 2000, wages of £50,000 a week for a footballer was still newsworthy and controversial. Players were earning far more in a week than most of us would do in a whole year. Roy Keane got his wage demands met by Manchester United and in April 2000 rewarded them with a highly amusing own goal which helped to knock United out of the Champions League at the hands of Real Madrid.

SUPPORT

If you could listen to one Elvis Presley song what would it be: Hound Dog, Blue Suede Shoes, Jailhouse Rock, Heartbreak Hotel, All Shook Up, Can't Help Falling in Love or Suspicious Minds? If it was up to the board at Arsenal, you'd get a rendition of 'THE WONDER OF YOU' which was an era when Elvis was all washed up as opposed to all shook up.

When Arsenal moved to Asburton Grove in 2006, they decided to follow the footsteps of Ross County and Port Vale by playing this tune in an attempt to create an un-official Arsenal anthem. All it did was re-enforce the reality that football was becoming poncy and watered down.

For decades, Liverpool and Celtic play 'YOU'LL NEVER WALK ALONE' as the fans join in and hold up their scarves. As do West Ham fans with 'I'M FOREVER BLOWING BUBBLES'. The concept with 'THE WONDER OF YOU' at the Emirates was to play a song that would become tradition before every game. In response, the fans would lift up their scarves and sing along to it. Some did, most didn't because it wasn't organic. A song needs to come from the terraces and then the club can react to that, but in this case 'THE WONDER OF YOU' was a pony tailed marketing executive's idea of what should represent Arsenal.

The wonder of who actually wants this shite played before every game was the real mystery - and the club stopped playing the song from around 2012-2013 as it never caught on. To be fair to the club they dropped the song when it became more than apparent that it was not of The Arsenal.

"WE LOVE YOU ARSENAL, WE DO, (repeat twice)
OH ARSENAL, WE LOVE YOU!"

One of the most common chants which is often sung in defiance by away fans when the team is on the end of a heavy defeat. Examples in recent years include the 2-8 at Old Trafford in 2011, the 1-5 at Anfield and the 0-6 at Stamford Bridge in 2014.

By this point in time, the reputation of Arsenal's away following had become the opposite of the much ridiculed home crowd in terms of passionate support. However, it is also sung at home regularly, though in pockets of support, rarely if ever by a whole stand.

3PM AT HIGHBURY

"SHE WORE, SHE WORE,
SHE WORE A YELLOW RIBBON,
SHE WORE A YELOW RIBBON,
IN THE MERRY MONTH OF MAY,
AND WHEN, I ASKED HER, WHY SHE WORE THAT RIBBON,
SHE SAID IT'S FOR THE ARSENAL,
AND WE'RE GOING WEMBLEY,
WEMBLEY, WEMBLEY,
WERE THE FAMOUS ARSENAL AND WE'RE GOING WEMBLEY"
(Yellow Ribbon)

She Wore sprung back into life in 2014 and 2015 when Arsenal won back to back FA Cups and ended an eight season barren patch. The three previous FA Cup wins had been at Cardiff when Wembley was under redevelopment. The She Wore song was used at Cardiff but it never suited the chant like Wembley did.

The She Wore song from the Western movie of the same name in 1949 - was itself a derivation of many similar themed arrangements with a woman wearing a yellow ribbon for various reasons. The yellow ribbon had also been used in military circles for marching songs.

As Gav @Shewore has noted - this song is primarily associated with Arsenal fans from the late 1970s, and the trio of cup visits in 1978, 1979 and 1980 all of which Arsenal wore yellow; the song was a late 1970s away staple.

WE'VE ONLY GOT ONE SONG

It has been alleged that we appropriated it with a yellow flourish from Manchester United's scarlet version in their earlier 1970s Wembley trip; maybe we did, but what is unquestionable is that the song was a Gooners rally cry.

It has now spawned a website, social media presence, a banner in the new stadium and a stylish range of merchandise, including the ubiquitous clock from the Clock End, Highbury. All are intelligent, self knowing references to the origins of the Arsenal song from the 1970s.

"SING YOUR HEARTS OUT FOR THE LADS"
(Guide Me, O Thou Great Jehovah)

As the title would suggest, a heartfelt plea letting the players hear how much the fans care. Rarely heard these days and certainly never at home.

**"COME ON ARSENAL,
COME ON ARSENAL"**
(Chant)

Sung when the team are finding breaking down the opposition difficult; or in an important game as anxiety creeps into the crowd. Used as a way to express to the players to up their game, and get the goal to break the deadlock.

**"SEND ARSENAL DOWN THE FIELD,
FOR ONE MORE GOAL,
NO OTHER TEAM CAN FIGHT HARDER THAN ,
THE BOYS IN RED AND WHITE,
NEVER LET THEIR GLORY FADE,
LONG MAY IT GLOW,
SO LET US ALL GIVE OUT WITH,
UP THE GUNNERS!
UP THE GUNNERS!
GOAL!"**
(Anchors Aweigh)

Anchors Aweigh was an American Navy song which first appeared in 1906. It began as a chant for the US Navy football team, but with a bit of alteration became a song for the whole US Navy. It was given fresh impetus especially in Britain as the song was performed with gusto in the 1945 Movie "Anchors Aweigh" which starred Frank Sinatra and Gene Kelly.

Altered into 'The Arsenal Club Supporters Song' by C Goodman in the late 1940s it appeared proudly in the first ever edition of the fanzine Gunflash in 1949 (yes, Gunflash really has been going for that long).

It was evidently sung regularly as Whittaker's team carried on the work of Chapman and Allison, winning the League twice and the FA cup. Indeed in February 1952 Burnley fans shamelessly re-used the Arsenal supporters club song for their own purposes to extol their players to greater heights.

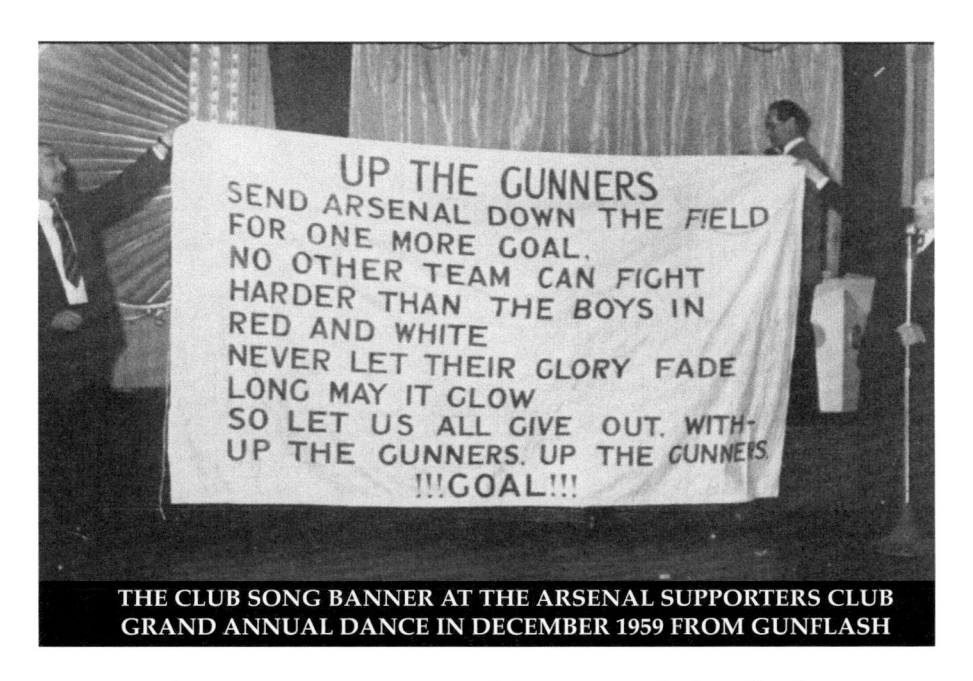

THE CLUB SONG BANNER AT THE ARSENAL SUPPORTERS CLUB GRAND ANNUAL DANCE IN DECEMBER 1959 FROM GUNFLASH

Despite being sung at Supporters Club events, including the above image from 1959, it had fallen out of favour at Highbury over the decade, because in 1963 the official match day programme printed the chant "which used to be heard on the ground some years ago" referring to it as "The Arsenal Song".

So keen were the club to re-introduce it that the Metropolitan Police Marching Band played it every game for the First Team from the 1963-64 season as their last tune before kick-off, which had been the policy a decade previously.

Uncharacteristically, the club were free and loose with the possibility of spending some cash. Saying of this song: "we shall be very happy to hear echoing and re-echoing from our stands… so let's hear all you budding singers and if you should lift the roof we shall be very happy to bear the cost of replacing it!"

However this had no effect and in 1965-66 Bob Wall the football club Secretary accepted that time had moved on and Arsenal needed a new song. The Arsenal it was said needed a modern tune and the club asked the Supporters club for assistance in devising a new one. The new song "Roll on the Arsenal" was premiered by the Metropolitan Police Band with their soloist in December 1965 before the match .

"ROLL ON THE ARSENAL,
LET'S HAVE A BARREL OF FUN,
ROLL ON THE ARSENAL,
WE'VE GOT THEM ALL ON THE RUN,
WIN ALL OUR MATCHES,
THEN WE'LL HAVE NOTHING TO FEAR,
1,2,3,4,5,6,7... AND THE GANG'S ALL HERE!"
(Roll Out the Barrel)

WE'VE ONLY GOT ONE SONG

It should come as no surprise that there is a distinct lack of evidence to suggest it found its way from the police band onto the Highbury terraces!!! Another attempt to popularise this song, in August 1967, led to the club asking for feedback from fans which was met by a scathing response from fans leaving Bob Wall in no doubt about their feelings of having a song foisted on them they did not want. The club, as with the Elvis song many years later, found that songs need to be organic and popular - or crowd led - to be taken up.

"IF YOU GO DOWN TO THE BRIDGE TODAY,
YOU'RE SURE OF A BIG SURPRISE,
IF YOU GO DOWN TO THE BRIDGE TODAY,
YOU'LL 'ARDLY BELIEVE YOUR EYES,
COS JEREMY THE SUGAR PUFF BEAR,
HAS BOUGHT SOME BOOTS AND CROPPED HIS HAIR,
'COS TODAY'S THE DAY,
THAT JEREMY JOINS THE SKINHEADS!"
(Teddy Bears' Picnic)

Before the Honey Monster, Jeremy The Bear was the face of Sugar Puffs and his Teddy Bears Picnic theme tune in the adverts 'IF YOU GO DOWN IN THE WOODS TODAY...' leant itself to this ditty, sung lustily from the North Bank in the later 1960s and 1970s.

Sung as a piss take, nearly all terraces had their own version, all slightly differing proclaiming Jeremy as the effete leader or member of an opposition crew. The North Bank version was based upon those that frequented the Kings Road and afterwards the Bridge.

There was much dispute amongst fans as to whether Jeremy's conversion to the Skinhead fraternity emanated in Chelsea or Portsmouth, or Bristol or Manchester or even on the North Bank!

"COME ON AND CHEER AGAIN,
FOR WE ARE HERE AGAIN, (repeat)
TO SEE THE GUNNERS STRIKE,
COME ON AND SCORE AGAIN,
WE WANNA ROAR AGAIN,
FOR YOU WILL NEVER BEAT,
THE BOYS IN RED AND WHITE,
LA LA LA LA LA LA LA LA LA!"

From the 1960s.

"YOU ARE MY ARSENAL,
MY ONLY ARSENAL,
YOU MAKE ME HAPPY,
WHEN SKIES ARE GREY,
YOU'LL NEVER KNOW JUST,
HOW MUCH I LOVE YOU,

DON'T EVER TAKE MY ARSENAL AWAY,
LA LA LA LA!"
(You are my sunshine)

You are my Sunshine was a US country song written in 1939 and which many artistes covered in the 1960s and 1970s. It was adapted all over the country, this one the version being sung by the Gunners.

"WE HATE NOTTINGHAM FOREST,
WE HATE LIVERPOOL TOO,
WE HATE TOTTENHAM HOTSPUR,
BUT ARSENAL WE LOVE YOU!"
(Land of Hope and Glory)

Could easily have different clubs - whatever took your fancy, but it had to scan! The primacy of Nottingham Forest would date this one to the early reign of Brian Clough and Peter Taylor circa late 1970s / early 1980s.

"WE ALL FOLLOW THE ARSENAL,
OVER LAND AND SEA... AND LEICESTER,
WE ALL FOLLOW THE ARSENAL, ON-TO VICTORY,
ALTOGETHER NOW" (repeat)
(Land of Hope and Glory)

An old song which to a degree has survived and is still occasionally heard at away games. The debating point on this song is when, or why, Leicester was added. There are two really compelling theories: on the way to the 1979 FA Cup final win, Arsenal was initially drawn against Sheffield Wednesday in the Third Round.

This took five ties to resolve and the last three games were played at Filbert Street in quick succession between 15 and 22 January. There were no Highbury games between 13 and 27 January so hard-core supporters were going to Filbert Street more often than Highbury for a couple of weeks, and many note this as the origin of the addition.

But another theory has it that it could also be due to the motorway sign which states 'To the North and Leicester' when travelling from London to the north. On reflection we go for the first theory, and believe all other team's fans who also use the "… and Leicester" element in their songs, did so only after hearing the Arsenal rendition.

"THE ARSENAL, THE ARSENAL, THE ARSENAL,
THE ARSENAL" (repeat)
(Chant)

Traditional old time chant, rarely heard these days. Indeed 'The Arsenal' is a phrase that is dying out with the black rhino. During an FA coaching seminar which Matt recently attended, the speaker Tom Youlden (FA Coach and former

Arsenal reserve player from the mid to late 1960s) kept on referring to 'The Arsenal' - much to the amusement of some of the younger audience members who couldn't understand the term.

It is a shame that the ignorance of these few meant they were unable to understand that 'The Arsenal' is not only the place of the origins of the club, but more importantly the legal name of the club. Matt made an attempt to explain to them that 'The Arsenal' is old fashioned but correct terminology - only to be ridiculed himself!! "Nah man, they don't say 'The Liverpool' or The Manchester United. In the league table it don't say 'The Arsenal'". God help us!!!!!

"GREEN, GREEN IS THE COLOUR FOR ME,
GREEN AS THE TURF AT WEMBLEY,
COS THAT IS WHERE, THE ARSENAL WILL BE,
FOR THE FA CUP IN 83!"
(Lord of the Dance)

In the 1982/83 season, Arsenal dropped yellow as the away colour and went green; a huge break from tradition. Back then, watching Arsenal play in green was as difficult to comprehend as accepting that Tony Woodcock cost the same amount to purchase as Lee Chapman in 1982.

The shirt had blue sleeves and the shorts were blue – which made the players look like overgrown ball boys at Wimbledon. They were also notoriously difficult for players to sight each other when on the pitch and the shirt only lasted a year after copious complaints from the team. In May 1983 the green turf at Wembley was not graced by Arsenal as hoped, and for the following season the club went back to...

"YEEEEEELLLLLLOOOOOOWWWWWWS"
(Chant)

That's what we want to hear at away games.

"GIMME DAT, GIMME DAT, GIMME DAT BANANA!"
(Gimme Dat Banana)

As Nottingham Forest played in an all yellow strip in 1977 they were serenaded by the North Bank's version of this late seventies one hit wonder by Black Gorilla.

"COME ON YOU REDS!"
(Chant)

Most likely a chant that begun in Woolwich, as "The Reds" was Arsenal's first nickname and it has been used ever since from the terraces. In the latter period at Highbury the scoreboard screens would start flashing these words when a corner was taken to extol the crowd to cheer the team on further. This was automatically sung whenever we were awarded a corner. It was the scoreboard screen which saw the beginning of the end for this chant, as no-one likes to be told what to sing.

**"LET IT BE, LET IT BE,
LA, LA, LA, LA, LA, LA, LA, LA, LA, ARSENAL"**

Sung on the North Bank after The Beatles released it in 1970.

"COME ON YOU GUNNERS!"
(Chant)

Out of favour, but often heard at Highbury, though as an individual shout not a collective chant.

**"WE ARE RED, WE ARE WHITE,
WE ARE FUCKING DYNAMITE, LA LA LA LA LA LA LA LA!"**
(The Caissons Go Rolling Along)

Another rarely heard old favourite loosely based around an American Army song.

**"MAYBE IT'S BECAUSE I'M A LONDONER,
THAT I LOVE LONDON TOWN,
MAYBE IT'S BECAUSE I'M A LONDONER,
THAT I THINK OF HER WHEREVER I GO,
I GET A FUNNY FEELING INSIDE OF ME,
JUST WALKING UP AND DOWN,
MAYBE IT'S BECAUSE I'M A LONDONER
THAT I LOVE LONDON TOWN"**
(Maybe It's Because I'm a Londoner)

Not all songs emanating from the terraces were about Arsenal, some such as this post war classic were sung by most sets of London fans. Written in 1947 it was performed originally in music hall style by Bud Flanagan.
Flanagan, incidentally the voice of the Dad's Army theme tune, was the Vice President of the Arsenal Supporters Club and regularly seen in Highbury - so the song did resonate with Gunners for that reason too.

**"BERTIE MEE SAID TO BILL SHANKLY,
HAVE YOU HEARD OF THE NORTH BANK HIGHBURY?
THE SHANKS SAID "YES,
THEY'RE THE LOUDEST AND THE BEST,
AND THEY ALL SUPPORT THE ARSE-NAL!"**
(Lord of the Dance)

One that was sung in reverse by the Scousers.

WE'VE ONLY GOT ONE SONG

"WHEN YOU'RE SMILING, WHEN YOU'RE SMILING,
THE WHOLE WORLD SMILES WITH YOU,
WHEN YOU'RE SMILING, WHEN YOU'RE SMILING,
THE SUN COMES SHINING THROUGH,
BUT WHEN YOU'RE CRYING, YOU BRING ON THE RAIN,
SO STOP YOU'RE CRYING, BE HAPPY AGAIN,
WHEN YOU'RE SMILING, WHEN YOU'RE SMILING,
THE WHOLE WORLD SMILES WITH YOU,
NA NA NA NA NA, THE WHOLE WORLD SMILES WITH YOU"
(When You're Smiling)

An inter war song first recorded by Louis Armstrong; it was also covered in the 1950s by Frank Sinatra and Dean Martin and the in the 1960s by Andy Williams. This is one of those that was not altered, but regularly got an airing at Highbury in the 1960s onwards.

"WALK ON THROUGH THE WIND,
WALK ON THROUGH THE RAIN,
THOUGH YOUR DREAMS BE TOSSED AND BLOWN,
WALK ON, WALK ON,
WITH HOPE IN YOUR HEART,
AND YOU'LL NEVER WALK ALONE,
YOU'LL NEVER WALK ALONE!"
(You'll Never Walk Alone)

In the 1960s and early 1970s this song was universal in football grounds, not just exclusive to Liverpool. It originated from the 1945 hit musical 'Carousel' and took off after a spate of mid 1960s pop versions.

It was sung by Gunners during the 1971 FA cup final just after Arsenal had equalised via Eddie Kelly in extra time, setting the team on their way to beating Liverpool and gaining the double.

Heard regularly on the North Bank where each line was punctuated with claps, this song fell away from Highbury around the time that Liverpool began to dominate the English game from the mid-1970s.

solo "GIVE ME A COCONUT"
all "COCONUT!"
solo "GIVE ME A COCONUT"
all "COCONUT!"
solo "GIVE ME A COCONUT"
all "COCONUT!"
solo "WHAT'VE YA GOT?"
all "I'VE GOT A LUVVERLY BUNCH OF COCONUTS,
ALL OF THEM STANDING IN A ROW,
BIG ONES, SMALL ONES,
SOME AS BIG AS YOUR HEAD!"
(I've got a lovely bunch of coconuts)

An amusing song written originally during WW2 it had some exposure in the late 1960s on television, hence its appearance on the North bank, despite it being a rather eccentric terrace song.

**"WE LOVE TO GO A WANDERING,
A WANDERING ON OUR WAY,
WE WANDER UP TO STOKE CITY,
AND HEAR THE NORTH BANK SA,Y
ARSENAL ARSENAL CHAMPIONS... ARSENAL CHAMPIONS!"**
(The Happy Wanderer)

**"WE'RE BETTER THAN UNITED,
AND WE'RE LOUDER THAN THE KOP,
WE'RE SECOND IN THE FOOTBALL LEAGUE,
WE'LL SOON BE AT THE TOP,
NA NA NA NA NA NA NA NA NA NA, NA NA NA NA NA NA NA NA!"**
(MOTD theme tune)

1971 as Arsenal catch up 'dirty Leeds'. Both these being sung around the double season

**"ROLL OUT THE RED CARPET, COS THE RED CARPET'S,
GONNA ROLL ROLL ROLL, RIGHT OVER THE LAND.
ROLL OUT THE RED CARPET, COS WE'LL GET STARTED
AND ROLL ROLL ROLL, TO WEMBLEY LAND!"**
(1978 FA Cup final song)

Despite being the team song of a losing final, this surprisingly catchy tune is often heard in and around Islington's pubs wherever Lee Gregory and his merry bunch of Gooners are drinking on match day.

**"AY YI YI YI,
WILSON IS BETTER THAN YASHIN,
STOREY IS BETTER THAN YASHIN,
AND SPURS ARE IN FOR A THRASHING!"**
(Cielito Lindo, AKA the Ay, Ay, Ay, Ay song)

Lev Yashin was a legendary USSR 'keeper who was world renowned during the 1960s.

**"IN DUBLIN'S FAIR CITY, WHERE THE GIRLS ARE SO PRETTY,
I FIRST SET MY EYES ON SWEET MOLLY MALONE,
AS SHE WHEELED HER WHEELBARROW,
THROUGH STREETS BROAD AND NARROW,
SINGING (PAUSE)
CLAP, CLAP, CLAP CLAP CLAP, CLAP CLAP CLAP CLAP, ARSENAL!"**
(Molly Malone)

An Irish folk song with an Arsenal twist, which these days has been truncated in the final banging line.

"ZIGGER ZAGGER, ZIGGER ZAGGER, OI OI OI"

Regularly chanted in the 60s

"WE ALL AGREE, ARSENAL ARE MAGIC"
(Cielito Lindo, AKA the Ay, Ay, Ay, Ay song)

A 'golden oldie' from the late 1960s, this is an adaptation of a very old Mexican song which was made popular by an American advert for crisps, which ran for a number of years from 1967 onwards, using Anglicised words to the tune of the "AY, AY, AY, AY" song.

**"WE'RE PROUD OF YOU, WE'RE PROUD OF YOU,
WE'RE PROUD OF YOU, ARSENAL!
WE'RE PROUD OF YOU, WE'RE PROUD OF YOU,
WE'RE PROUD OF YOU, ARSENAL."**
(Auld Lang Syne)

Back in the day if the team had performed well but succumbed to defeat.

**"ONE TEAM IN LONDON,
THERE'S ONLY ONE TEAM IN LONDON…"**
(Guantanamera)

And it ain't Middlesex Hotspur

**"SCORE IN A MINUTE… WE'RE GONNA SCORE IN A MINUTE,
SCORE IN A MINUTE… WE'RE GONNA SCORE IN A MINUTE."**
(Guantanamera)

"ALL WE ARE SAYING… IS GIVE US A GOAL!"
(Give Peace a Chance)

Sung at the end of the GG reign when goals were on occasion hard to come by, despite Wrightie being on the pitch

"GEORGIE, GEORGIE, SORT 'EM OUT, GEORGIE, SORT 'EM OUT"

Sung at half time when the team needed a GG rocket to improve

"THEO, THEO, GIVE US A BALL!"

The North Bank, sung to George Graham's assistant, Theo Foley.

"WE WILL WIN, WE WILL WIN, WE WILL WIN"
(Stars and Stripes)

Heard when the team was creating chances but not in a winning position.

"ARSENAL ARE BACK, HELLO, HELLO"
(Chant)

Memorably sung in the late 1980s as George Graham re-invigorated the club. It was later heard in February 1992 when Arsenal spanked Sheffield Wednesday 7-1 at Highbury. Graham's men up to that point had put up a poor defence of the league title and had been knocked out of the FA Cup by Fourth Division Wrexham. On this afternoon in 1992, something clicked and the Arsenal from the year before were back as they tore Wednesday apart.

Arsenal remained unbeaten for the rest of the season and played the best free flowing football of the George Graham era. It was too late to get back in title race, or to finishing third to qualify for Europe (pipped by, of all teams, Sheffield Wednesday) but the team were so impressive that, for the 1992/93 season, they were made favourites for the title, however, Graham went more defensive and would shine in the cups instead of the league.

**"ATTACK, ATTACK,
ATTACK, ATTACK, ATTACK"**
(Chant)

Anfield 1989, deep into the second half, one goal to win the title and the away end were literally chanting for all out attack. The second goal came and the title was won – not on goal difference – but on goals scored. Despite myths and perceptions, the truth was that George Graham's first years in charge produced high goal rates - but that did change near the end of his tenure. That leads us onto the chant most associated with the Arsenal.

**"ONE NIL,
TO THE ARSENAL,
ONE NIL,
TO THE ARSENAL"**
(Go West)

Another huge favourite, this first made an appearance in the European Cup Winners Cup campaign of 1993/94. It started at the First Leg of the Cup Winners Cup semi final at the Parc des Princes on 29 March 1994. Arsenal fan Kelvin Meadows recalls "the PSG fans, known as the Boulogne Boys, started singing along to 'Go West' with what sounded like 1-0! So we joined in and sang "1-0 TO THE ARSENAL". Though the song quickly ended in this particular game as Ginola equalised soon after the break.

The home leg Semi-Final was won 1-0, where the chant circulated around the Clock End when Kevin Campbell scored the only goal of the game. The following weekend, Arsenal played Chelsea at Highbury, and before the game, Ian Wright addressed the crowd on the big TV screens and said that although he was gutted to be missing the final – he'd be in Copenhagen to cheer the team on. He then started singing '1-0 To the Arsenal' to the tune of 'Go West' and that's when the chant really caught momentum with the whole crowd. That afternoon Arsenal beat Chelsea 1-0. A month later, in one of the greatest moments in the club's history, the European Cup Winners' Cup was won fittingly in the final - 1-0 with a Smudger first half goal against Parma. Taken from the Pet Shop Boys September 1993 cover of the original Village People song, it quickly became the anthem of the remainder of George Graham's managerial career at Arsenal; which events conspired to ensure was not too long.

One thing to note, is that although the 1-0 chant is now firmly associated with the Graham era, it wasn't heard until 1994; eight years into his nine year reign as manager. This one is still given an airing regularly today.

**"TERRY NEILL'S, RED AND WHITE ARMY,
TERRY NEILL'S, RED AND WHITE ARMY"**
(Chant)

Sung through many games in the 1970s and 1980s

"GEORGIE GRAHAM'S, RED AND WHITE ARMY…"
(Chant)

Sung through many games in the 1980s or early 1990s. Adapted later to:

"ARSENE WENGER'S, RED AND WHITE ARMY…'
with the-add on **"WE HATE TOTTENHAM!".**

All chants were repeated as many times as required

**"WE'RE THE NORTH BANK,
WE'RE THE NORTH BANK,
WE'RE THE NORTH BANK, HIGHBURY!"**
(Military chant)

This chant came about after the North Bank was renamed from the Laundry End by the fans in circa 1966. Those involved in the name change said it was for the simple reason that it was easier to sing about the North Bank than the Laundry End.

The terrace built initially in 1913, was called the Laundry End or the Gillespie Road End as it was on Gillespie Road and in the street behind the terrace stood the Mayfield Laundry.

**"WE'RE THE NORTH BANK, WE'RE THE NORTH BANK,
WE'RE THE NORTH BANK, HIGHBURY!
WE'RE THE CLOCK END, WE'RE THE CLOCK END,**

NORTH BANK WRITTEN ON A BANNER IN JANUARY 1967 AT BRISTOL, CHARLIE GEORGE CAN BE SEEN BELOW THE 'N' OF NORTH BANK

>WE'RE THE CLOCK END, HIGHBURY!
>WE'RE THE NORTH BANK, WE'RE THE NORTH BANK,
>WE'RE THE NORTH BANK, HIGHBURY!
>WE'RE THE CLOCK END, WE'RE THE CLOCK END,
>WE'RE THE CLOCK END, HIGHBURY!"

The circular chanting back and forth between the respective terraces came afterwards. It is interesting that at the new stadium the same song is chanted with no deviation. It is still Highbury a decade after the move.

>"WE'RE THE TOPSIDE, WE'RE THE TOPSIDE,
>WE'RE THE TOPSIDE, OVER HERE"

>"WE'RE THE MIDDLE, WE'RE THE MIDDLE,
>WE'RE THE MIDDLE, OVER HERE"

The North Bank even had its own intra-terrace songs denoting different territory depending where you stood on its steps.

>"SIGN HIM UP, SIGN HIM UP, SIGN HIM UP,
>SIGN HIM UP, SIGN HIM UP"
>(Stars and Stripes Forever)

WE'VE ONLY GOT ONE SONG

Before the start of the Villa Game in May 1981 Pele, the Brazilian legend, who was a guest at Highbury, was introduced to the crowd and received a massive round of applause with many in the North Bank hinting to Terry Neill of the need to bolster the team line up.

"GOOD OLD ARSENAL,
WE'RE PROUD TO SAY THAT NAME,
AND WHILE WE SING THIS SONG,
WE'LL WIN THE GAME!"
(Rule Britannia)

Quite possibly the most iconic and recognisable Arsenal song together with '1-0 to the Arsenal'. Written by football commentator Jimmy Hill to accompany 'The Arsenal' for the 1971 FA Cup final. ITV held a competition for an Arsenal song but none matched Jimmy's expectations so he penned it himself.

The Arsenal team recorded "GOOD OLD ARSENAL" and the song peaked at number 16 in the UK singles chart. Consequently, Arsenal were the first club side to have a hit single. It was quickly taken to by fans as it is a jovial and easy to learn club anthem. Quite recently the club has seen sense and play this classic before games. In 2015 an Unofficial Arsenal FA Cup record was released - by the Riders of the Night and a group of "Friends", it raised money for Bob Wilson's Willow Foundation and was a clever mash up of "GOOD OLD ARSENAL", "OOH TO BE A GOONER" and "WE'RE ON OUR WAY".

"ONE MICHAEL WATSON,
THERE'S ONLY ONE MICHAEL WATSON,
ONE MICHAEL WATSON"
(Guantanemera)

In 1991 the boxer Michael 'The Force' Watson lost to Chris Eubank at White Hart Lane in one of the greatest - and most tragic fights in British boxing history. A proud Gooner, Watson wore Arsenal colours to his bouts and also had a large Arsenal fan following in the stands. Watson dominated Eubank for 10 rounds, but was then was knocked down in the 11th and stopped in the 12th. A resulting blood clot nearly took his life and he would spend the following few years paralysed. In 1993 Arsenal held a benefit match for Watson: Arsenal v Tottenham featured former players such as Michael Thomas, who was booed because of moving to Anfield, and Watson was wheeled out on to the pitch as the crowd chanted his name. In 2002, Watson not only fought his way out of the wheelchair, but he walked the London Marathon.

"COME ON YOU RIP ROARING REDS, COME ON YOU RIP ROARING, GOAL SCORING GUNNERS!"

A lone fan located in East stand would chant "Come on you Rip Roaring Reds" to accompany the start of a game and indeed whenever he fancied to bellow out his eccentric lines. He became known as Rip Roar owing to his self-styled chant, and these stickers were produced in recognition by the OpAa Artists, Dan McCarthy and Michael Henry.

On occasion the North Bank would implore him to pipe up with chants of:

"RIP ROAR, RIP ROAR, GIVE US A SONG, RIP ROAR, GIVE US A SONG"

To which Rip-Roar, when present in the ground, would oblige with a full throated rendition.

"RIP-ROAR IS A WANKER, RIP-ROAR IS A WANKER LA, LA, LA, LA"

Some though were less amused by Rip-Roar's admittedly limited repertoire, though he did branch out occasionally into a variation adding "Goal Scoring Gunners".

"GIVE ME AN A	(lead solo)
A	(crowd)
GIVE ME AN R	(lead solo)
R	(crowd)
GIVE ME AN S	(lead solo)
S	(crowd)
GIVE ME AN E	(lead solo)
E	(crowd)
GIVE ME AN N	(lead solo)
N	(crowd)
GIVE ME AN A	(lead solo)
A	(crowd)
GIVE ME AN L	(lead solo)
L	(crowd)
PUT 'EM ALL TOGETHER AND WHAT HAVE YOU GOT?	(lead solo)
THE ARSENAL, THE ARSENAL, THE ARSENAL..."	(crowd)

A chant sung as individual letters to make up the whole of the Arsenal. On occasion the 'E' was elongated and there was clapping between "The Arsenal".

WE'VE ONLY GOT ONE SONG

Often the final line from the lead soloist would ask a different question such as "WHO'S GONNA WIN THE FOOTBALL LEAGUE?" depending how well the team was doing at the time. Not just a great chant - but also a good spelling lesson.

**"YOU'RE NOT SINGING ANYMORE,
YOU'RE NOT SINGING ANYMORE!"**
(Guide Me, O Thou Great Jehovah)

Usually given an airing if the opponents have just shipped a goal, and a previously boisterous set of fans have been quiet for a few minutes. Sometimes it backfires and it never looks good when the fans who have sung it had previously been quiet.

For example, in the second competitive game at the Emirates Stadium in 2006, Dynamo Zagreb took the lead to the delight of their partisan away support, who despite only having numbers of 1,000 filled the stadium with noise. Arsenal equalised and the home fans piped up with "YOU'RE NOT SINGING ANYMORE" – until they realised that Zagreb fans were still singing – and still drowning out the other 57,418.

"WE'LL SUPPORT YOU EVERMORE!"
(Guide Me, O Thou Great Jehovah)

This was heard in the terracing years – when the team were going through rough times but giving it their all. The era of the supporter – not the fan who now buys a ticket to be entertained. It's no coincidence that songs like this one faded away when ticket prices sky rocketed. When fans ended up paying so much just to watch a game they felt cheated when they didn't get what they wanted. When it costs a day's wages to watch a game, people tend to get fussy about what they're watching.

**"ON THE FIRST DAY OF CHRISTMAS MY TRUE LOVE GAVE TO ME,
PAT JENNINGS IN OUR GOAL,
ON THE SECOND DAY OF CHRISTMAS MY TRUE LOVE GAVE TO ME,
2 PAT RICE AND PAT JENNINGS IN OUR GOAL,
ON THE THIRD DAY OF CHRISTMAS MY TRUE LOVE GAVE TO ME,
3 SAMMY NELSON, 2 PAT RICE AND PAT JENNINGS IN OUR GOAL,
ON THE FOURTH DAY OF CHRISTMAS MY TRUE LOVE GAVE TO ME,
4 BRIAN TALBOT, 3 SAMMY NELSON, 2 PAT RICE
AND PAT JENNINGS IN OUR GOAL!"**
(Twelve Days of Christmas)

To the tune of the Christmas carol 'Twelve Days of Christmas' player number 5 was David O'Leary – who was the Partridge in a Pear Tree. This song went on to include at 6 Willie Young; 7 Chippie Brady; 8 Alan Sunderland; 9 Frank Stapleton; 10 David Price and 11 Graham Rix.

This song can't get adapted to today's team because the player shirt numbering goes higher than the amount of years it's been since Spurs last won the title. 'On the third day of Christmas My True Love Gave To Me – 23 Danny Welbeck' isn't going to work out.

Not to mention that squads are so much bigger than back in the late 1970s and early 1980s; the song would have to be changed for every game. In the 1979-80 season, Arsenal played 70 matches with little in the way of squad rotation. Brian Talbot played in every single game and what with getting to the final of two cup competitions - at one stage the team played four games in one week. What was that about players today needing a winter break?

"YOU DON'T KNOW WHAT YOU'RE DOING!"

Usually directed towards a referee or manager.

"THE REFEREE'S A WANKER!"

Definitely sung to the referee.

"SPANISH, AND YOU KNOW YOU ARE!"
(Go West)

To the Catalonians of Barcelona – a group of people who never like to be referred to as Spanish due to their ongoing struggle for self determination.

"RED ARMY, RED ARMY"

A staple at the Ashburton Ground. Sung over and over again as many times as fans wish to. It's quite easy to remember the words! One of Mark's favourites, who remembers this first being corrupted to "REG VARNEY" (from On The Buses TV show) in 1991 as we were walking out of Stamford Bridge after our single League defeat in the 1990/91 season.

"UNAI EMERY'S RED AND WHITE ARMY."
(Chant)

"WE'VE GOT OUR ARSENAL BACK."
(Those were the days)

Both heard often and loud during the away games in the 22 game unbeaten run in 2018/19 campaign. Specifically the 'We've got our Arsenal back' was chanted after the 5-1 rout at Craven Cottage in October 2018 during this unbeaten run.

RIVALS

We hate Tottenham, but who comes after that, or even before that as the team we love to hate more than anyone? Without doubt, Chelsea are a contender, and for some, Manchester United will always be our most despised foe. Arsenal and Liverpool's rivalry has mellowed somewhat in the last two decades, but during the 1970s and 1980s things were a lot more heated.

The North / South divide is derived from the Industrial Revolution. Using this helpful stereotype, the North is the land of coal, factories, shipbuilding, the dole and Coronation Street. Obviously it is not the whole truth and these days just a very small aspect of it, but it's still great for the thinking up of songs about our football rivals from the north, and these songs are better if based on stereotypes and not reality. Of the Northern sides, Liverpool was singled out as being primarily dole claimants, always on the rob for your hubcaps or whatever else that was not nailed down!

It must be remembered that no stereotype can exist without being based on a germ of truth, and Gooner football chants thrived certainly in the 1970s to 1990s on these perceived notions of the northerner.

> "IN YOUR LIVERPOOL SLUMS, (Repeat once)
> YOU LOOK IN THE DUSTBIN FOR SOMETHING TO EAT,
> YOU FIND A DEAD RAT AND YOU THINK IT'S A TREAT,
> IN YOUR LIVERPOOL SLUMS"
> (In Our Liverpool Home by the Spinners)

This was not specifically an Arsenal anti-Liverpool song; it was sung all over the country especially virulently as the Scousers cleaned up between the mid 1970s to the late 1980s. But the fact that it was probably devised by another set of fans - didn't stop it being sung by Gunners to Liverpool both home and away.

The above lyrics were quite ironic as the song this chant was taken from - was a pro-Liverpool Spinners folk song called "In your Liverpool homes" of cloying sentimentality released in 1962, which did not lend itself to the rest of the country - hence the inversion of the original meaning. Ironically the 2nd verse of the original Spinners song appears to approve of stealing!

This was also sung to anyone outside of North London. In the days when things were more localised you'd hear a variation on the same chant to fans in other parts of London. In your West London slums!

"WE HATE BILL SHANKLEY,
AND WE HATE THE KOP,
WE'LL FIGHT MAN UNITED UNTIL WE DROP,
WE DON'T GIVE A WIGGLE,
AND WE DON'T GIVE A WANK,
WE ARE THE ARSENAL, NORTH BANK!"
(Lord of the Dance)

"SIGN ON, SIGN ON,
WITH A PEN IN YOUR HAND,
AND YOU'LL NE-VER, GET, A JOB,
YOU'LL NE-VER GET, A JOB,
SIGN ON, SIGN ON"
(You'll Never Walk Alone)

Any Liverpool fan offended by this, now knows how we felt when we were subjected to the Anfield Rap. For those who don't remember the Anfield Rap - do not look it up on Youtube. However, on occasions, the scousers did show a sense of humour and they replied with this chant:

'THANK YOU VERY MUCH FOR SIGNING OUR GIROS,
THANK YOU VERY MUCH,
THANK YOU VERY, VERY, VERY, MUCH'
('Thank You Very Much')

Which was also a tune in a series of 1980s Roses chocolate adverts, which used this Scaffold song which originally charted in 1967.

'YOU'RE JUST A SCOUSER,
A DIRTY SCOUSER,
YOU'RE ONLY HAPPY, ON GIRO DAY,
YOUR MUM'S OUT STEALING,
YOUR DAD'S DRUG DEALING,
OH PLEASE DON'T TAKE MY HUB CAPS AWAY!'
(You are my Sunshine)

"WHERE'S YOUR FAMOUS ATMOSPHERE?"
(Guide me Oh thou great Jehovah)

To Liverpool at Anfield when their famed wit and songs don't transpire.

"HAND IT OVER LIVERPOOL"
(Guide me, O Thou Great Jehovah)

Sung during the 1988/89 and 1990/91 seasons, when Arsenal won the title and Liverpool were, on both occasions, the defending champions. This chant was changed to 'HAND IT OVER MANCHESTER' in 1998.

WE'VE ONLY GOT ONE SONG

"WE WON THE LEAGUE, ON MERSEYSIDE,
WE WON THE LEAGUE ON ,
WE WON THE LEAGUE ON THE MERSEY,
WE WON THE LEAGUE ON MERSEYSIDE"
(When the Saints Go Marching In)

The 1989 vintage, but not heard so often anymore because in 2002 this happened:

"WE WON THE LEAGUE, AT MANCHESTER,
WE WON THE LEAGUE AT MANCHESTER,
WE WON THE LEAGUE AT OLD TRAFFORD,
WE WON THE LEAGUE AT MANCHESTER"
(When The Saints Go Marching In)

Which before 2002 was preceded by:

"OH MANCHESTER, IS FULL OF SHIT,
OH MANCHESTER IS FULL OF SHIT,
IT'S FULL OF SHIT, SHIT, AND MORE SHIT,
OH MANCHESTER IS FULL OF SHIT!"
(When The Saints Go Marching In)

Arsenal have won the League title at Man United 2002; Tottenham 1971 and 2004; Liverpool in 1989; Chelsea in 1933 and 1934; Middlesbrough in 1935, and Huddersfield in 1948. We have also won it on six occasions at Highbury, while only Villa has won it at on our ground, and even then they lost the game in 1981.

"WE'LL WIN THE LEAGUE, IN MANCHESTER,
WE'LL WIN THE LEAGUE IN MANCHESTER,
WE'LL WIN THE LEAGUE IN MANCHESTER,
WE'LL WIN AT OLD TRAFFORD,
WE'LL WIN THE LEAGUE IN MANCHESTER"
(When The Saints Go Marching In)

"FUCK ALL, FUCK ALL, FUCK ALL, UNITED WILL WIN FUCK ALL,
WHILE THE COCKNEY REDS ARE GOING OUT OF THEIR HEADS,
MAN UNITED WILL WIN FUCK ALL'
(The Entertainer)

"WE SHALL NOT, WE SHALL NOT BE MOVED,
WE SHALL NOT, WE SHALL NOT BE MOVED,
LIKE THE TEAM THAT'S GONNA WIN THE FOOTBALL LEAGUE,
WE SHALL NOT BE MOVED"
(We Shall Not Be Moved)

**"HAND IT OVER, HAND IT OVER,
HAND IT OVER FERGUSON"**
(Guide me, O Thou Great Redeemer)

"THERE'S ONLY ONE HARRY CRAWFORD"

All these above five songs were sung at the Old Trafford 2002 game. They were chanted variously before the game; during the game; at half time for the penalty competition winner, Harry Crawford, who was representing Arsenal.

"SEE YOU, ON THE MOTORWAY"
(Go West)

Sung regularly at Old Trafford; Manchester United fans coming from London has provided much in the way of mockery.

"YOU'LL BE HOME IN TEN MINUTES"
(Guide me, O Thou Great Jehovah)

Sung at Highbury to the Cockney Reds.

**"USA, USA,
USA, USA,
USA, USA,
USA, USA!"**
(USA)

Sung to Manchester United fans incessantly in and after the 2005 FA Cup final as the Glazers, an American family, had just taken over at Old Trafford. A sarcastic reference to the bovine chant adopted by followers of international American teams particularly in the Ryder Cup (or directed to any Presidential candidate before they bugger the country up). It appears to have come back to bite us. In recent years, as in the intervening years, Arsenal have acquired an American owner who's as popular as rabies. Incidentally, 'USA' was also chanted in the away end by Shalke 04 fans at Highbury in 2001. It had followed a minutes silence for the victims of the 911 World Trade Centre attacks.

**"THE LEAGUE,
WE HOPE YOU WIN THE LEAGUE"**
(Blue Moon)

Arsenal fans have little love for Aston Villa, and many refer to them as the 'Spurs' of the midlands. In 1981 the team in Claret and Blue won the league at Highbury and brawls between rival mobs broke out on the pitch before and more specifically after the game. However, Gooner dislike for Manchester United is at a far higher level - and in 1993 Villa and United were battling it out for the league title in a two horse race.

Arsenal fans rather enjoyed the fact that United hadn't won the league since 1967 and wanted it to stay that way. Villa came to Highbury and won 1-0 with a Tony Daley header. The Clock End didn't seem that upset with the result, and after the game ended chanted songs to the Villa fans in a very – very – rare show of good will shown towards opposition fans.

"MANCHESTER, WANK WANK WANK,
MANCHESTER, WANK WANK WANK,
MANCHESTER, WANK WANK WANK!"
(Chant)

A ditty for either United or City.

"WE'RE SO PRETTY,
WE HATE MAN CITY,
WE'RE VIOLENT!"
(Pretty Vacant by the Sex Pistols)

Sex Pistols front man John Lydon was delighted with this one. Hailing from Finsbury Park, the epicentre of Arsenal Land, Lydon has been a fan since the 1960s and now watches the games from his home in LA. When back in London, he generally watches games at the pub rather than at the new stadium, which he has described as looking like a modern bus station.

"DIVISION TWO IS CALLING YOU,
DOO DAH, DOO DAH,
DIVISION TWO IS CALLING YOU,
DOO DAH, DOO DAH DAY"

"£30 A WEEK, £30 POUND A WEEK,
DOO DAH, DOO DAH,
£30 A WEEK, £30 POUND A WEEK!
DOO DAH DOO DAH DAY"
(Camptown Races)

Sung at Maine Road in 1987 when City were heading for relegation to Division Two (Renamed 'League One' and then 'The Championship'). Arsenal fan TP recalls the chant: "The City fans didn't really get it, we were celebrating their predicament in their team's relegation and their fans social standing as £28/£30 was dole money for the time. All they saw was cockney twats singing, dancing and doing the conga while their team was 3-0 down"

"IS THERE A FIRE DRILL?
IS THERE A FIRE DRILL?
IS THERE A FIRE DRILL?"
(La Donna e Mobile - Verdi)

TO ARSENAL

3PM SATURDAY AT HIGHBURY

3 P

On the final away game of the 2015-2016 season, Manchester City fans left the ground at the end of the 2-2 draw like there was a fire drill rather than waiting to hear Manuel Pellegrini give his farewell speech. As it was, Pellegrini spoke to a 75% empty stadium.

"YOU'RE THE SHIT OF MANCHESTER"
(Guide me, Thou O Great Jehovah)

Sung to Manchester City fans in the years (decades) when they were the second best team in the city of Manchester. In other words, for most of the years before the oil money came rolling in.

**"SILVERWARE NO SILVERWARE,
YOU STILL AIN'T GOT NO SILVERWARE,
FROM STAMFORD BRIDGE TO ANYWHERE,
YOU STILL AIN'T GOT NO SILVERWARE!"**
(Red Flag)

Oh how we miss singing this one. Arsenal fans under a certain age will never have had the pleasure of reminding Chelsea fans that their trophy cabinet had less use than Ken Bates' electric fence. To put it in very simple terms, Chelsea between the mid-1970s and mid-1990s – were shit.

**"MILLWALL WITH MONEY,
YOU'RE ONLY MILLWALL WITH MONEY,
MILLWALL WITH MONEY"**
(Guantanamera)

Trophy insults had to make way for explanations as to why Chelsea were now getting the better of us on the pitch.

**BUILD A BONFIRE, (Repeat once)
PUT THE TOTTENHAM ON THE TO,P
PUT THE CHELSEA IN THE MIDDLE,
AND WE'LL BURN THE FUCKING LOT"**
(Darling Clementine)

**"STAMFORD BRIDGE IS FALLING DOWN,
FALLING DOWN, FALLING DOWN,
STAMFORD BRIDGE IS FALLING DOWN,
FUCK OFF CHELSEA,
BUILD IT UP IN RED AND WHITE,
RED AND WHITE, RED AND WHITE,
BUILD IT UP IN RED AND WHITE,
FUCK OFF CHELSEA"**
(London Bridge is Falling Down)

"YOU'RE NOT CHELSEA ANYMORE"
(Guide me, Thou O Great Jehovah)

Sung by away fans at Stamford Bridge in 2005, which made note of the change and gentrification of the modern day Chelsea home crowd.

**"CAREFREE, WHEREVER YOU MAY BE,
CHELSEA SCORED TWO BUT KANU SCORED THREE"**
(Lord of the Dance)

Chelsea v Arsenal; Stamford Bridge in October 1999. Two goals from Tore Andre Flo and Dan Petrescu put Chelsea 2-0 up before half time, and they were cruising to an easy win. But Kanu had different ideas and his hat-trick enabled the Gooners to subvert this Chelsea chant to goad the blues with.

**"SHIT CLUB NO HISTORY,
I'M A GOONER BABY,
AND I HATE THE CHELSEA"**
(Loser by Beck)

"GET YOUR MASCOT OFF THE PITCH"
(Guide me, Thou O Great Jehovah)

Chanted to Denis Wise, who was never a favourite of any opposing fan.
Regarding a related incident, a fellow vertically challenged Chelsea player from the late 1990s, Jody Morris, was standing near the section of Arsenal fans at Stamford Bridge, warming up as a sub, when the ball was kicked in his general direction and out of play.
"What you just standing there for, get the fucking ball, do your job" shouted one Arsenal fan.
"I'm a footballer, not a fucking ball boy" Says Jody.
"Are you, I've never seen you play before, you look more like a fucking ball boy" was the response.

**"HAVE YOU EVER SEEN CHELSEA PLAY LIKE THAT (Repeat twice)
HAVE YOU FUCK"**
(She'll be Coming Round the Mountain)

Not a song to be proud of, though very commonly heard from 2005 onwards when Chelsea were wining trophies and Arsenal were playing cavalier football - but winning as many trophies as Kim Jong-ill was winning Nobel Peace Prizes. The song made Arsenal fans sound like Spurs and West Ham excuse merchants. When Arsenal were winning league titles under George Graham - Spurs fans would try and take the high ground by claiming that they played prettier football. Hammers fans have always talked about playing football the 'West Ham way' which is a way that has resulted in no league titles and multiple relegations.

"YOU'RE NOT SPECIAL,
YOU'RE NOT SPECIAL,
YOU'RE NOT SPECIAL, YOU'RE A C*NT,
(Guide me Oh thou great Jehovah)

OK so this one was during his stint at Man Utd but no one really sees him as anything other than a Chelsea manager. Heard most notably and loudly during a 1-1 draw at Old Trafford in November 2016. Jose Mourinho has always referred to himself as the 'Special One'. Arsenal fans have always referred to him as something else.

"FUCK OFF MOURINHO!"
(La Donna e Mobile – Verdi)

Also heard in November 2016, but to be fair it appeared in any game against Chelsea when he was their manager.

"IS THIS THE EMIRATES?
"IS THIS THE EMIRATES?
"IS THIS THE EMIRATES?"
(La Donna e Mobile – Verdi)

During the first Arsenal match at the London Stadium, West Ham fans were serenaded with this song in December 2016. Reminding the Hammers of their recent painful loss of Upton Park, and in doing so re-iterating the little regard that the away support have for our current home.

"YOUR GROUND'S A COUNCIL HOUSE,
YOUR GROUND'S A COUNCIL HOUSE,
YOUR GROUND'S A COUNCIL HOUSE"
(La Donna e Mobile – Verdi)

At the same game and on the same theme, the Hammers were reminded that their ground had been paid for by the taxpayer, and not themselves.

"YOU DIRTY NORTHERN BASTARDS"

Self explanatory chant that Arsenal and all Southern clubs use to all and sundry Northerners.

"WE FORGOT THAT YOU WERE HERE!"
(Chant)

To an opposition support who had been quiet, or who had recently piped up.

"I GO DOWN PUB, DRINK TEN PINTS,
I GET REALLY PLASTERED,

**I GO BACK 'OME, AND BEAT MY WIFE ,
COS I'M A NORTHERN BASTARD!"**
(Hooray Hooray It's a Holi-Holiday – Boney M)

Sung specifically at Boro fans in the late 80s and 90s whilst putting on a fake Northern accent.

**"CAN YOU HEAR THE TOTTENHAM SING? NO, NO, (repeat once)
CAN YOU HEAR THE TOTTENHAM SING?
I CAN'T HEAR A FUCKING THING, WOAH, WOAH!"**

Of course this jibe could be for any opponent that had been quiet during a match. So we could have had Scousers (covering both Liverpool and Everton), Chelsea, Forest and a whole host of other teams rather than Spurs.

"LIVERPOOL WON FUCK ALL"
(Chant)

When Arsenal won the league at Old Trafford in 2002 it's important to remember that United were not the biggest threat to us in the title race that season. Liverpool were. So at the double winning party at Highbury a few days later against Everton in a 4-2 win – the Clock End did a parody of the annoying and droning 'LIVERPOOL, LIVERPOOL" that is usually heard coming out of the Kop. Initially, the Everton away fans didn't realise that the words had been slightly changed and looked bemused at the Clock End for singing a Liverpool chant. Then when it clicked what was being sung, they laughed and applauded the home fans!

**"THE WHEELS ON YOUR HOUSE GO ROUND AND ROUND,
ROUND AND ROUND, ROUND AND ROUND,
THE WHEELS ON YOUR HOUSE GO ROUND AND ROUND,
ALL THROUGH THE TOWN"**
(The Wheels On The Bus)

A recent staple at Stoke City or is it Storc City?

**"FUCK EM ALL, FUCK EM ALL,
UNITED, WEST HAM, LIVERPOOL,
'CAUSE WE ARE THE ARSENAL,
AND WE ARE THE BEST,
WE ARE THE ARSENAL, SO FUCK ALL THE REST,
FUCK EM ALL"**
(Bless Them All)

Originally a military corruption of a song popularised in World War Two, it was the theme to the 1961 film 'The Long and the Short and the Tall'; this Arsenal version is a fitting way to end the chapter.

SPURS

Other than the 'Players' and 'Support' chapters, welcome to the longest chapter of the book! That does speak volumes on how much attention we like to pay to that lot down the other end of Seven Sisters Road; bitter rivalry combined with mockery; most of the chants aimed at Tottenham combine the two. Spurs and Arsenal just don't get on as neighbours.

No religion involved like Rangers and Celtic. No inter-city rivalry such as Liverpool v Manchester United or Feyenoord v Ajax. No class differentiation like Flamingo v Fluminense or Inter v AC Milan. Just fans from the same neighbourhood, that went to the same schools – who simply cannot stand one another's football team.

Let us preface the following chants by saying that when Arsenal fans use the term 'Yiddo' or 'Yids', they're referring to Spurs football club fans, of any racial or religious backgrounds, who call and called themselves Yids. These chants are not directed at the Jewish community and contain no hatred of the religion, but of the Middlesex football team and their supporters.

However in the past on occasion things got out of hand and the club got involved and put a lid on it: In February 1987 the programme noted that against Tottenham in the League Cup semi final at Highbury there was "repeated violently abusive anti-Semitic chants - and we also had to remove provocative and offensive banners. The people who chanted those obscenities and brought those banners to the ground are a disgrace and an embarrassment to our club, and to our huge majority of well-behaved supporters. We don't want you in our stadium"

The past is another country; they do things differently there – is a great adage to use for all aspects of football in general and specifically the stopping of certain songs that were rife in the 70s and 80s. On occasions if obnoxious songs or chants were tried that the majority found unsavoury on this subject they were met with a retort of "YOU'RE JUST A BUNCH OF WANKERS" from their fellow fans.

Most normal people realise that racism is not an acceptable form of behaviour, and racism in general has reduced since the mid-1970s, owing in the main to policing and general societal changes.

Some songs or chants are near the knuckle and some go to the extremes; for example the escalator song which you will come across in the following chapter is in extremely bad taste - but has no religious or racial overtones. The context of the chant is all important for instance, it may or may not be acceptable to chant about 'Yids', depending largely on the recipient or how or what is being sung. As the Jewish Chronicle editor Stephen Pollard said "if offence isn't meant by those singing the word 'Yid', and if none is taken by those towards it is being sung, then how can racial hatred be involved?"

Arsenal has as many Jewish fans as Spurs and on balance we are not going to print the 'Yid' songs. We thought long and hard and wanted to keep this as a positive experience. While there are a few dodgy and borderline expressions in some songs there is no inclusion of songs that could be construed as anti-Semitic.

If you know them you know them; such as the Archibald song, the Clemence song and tiptoeing through the Paxton, to name but three examples. However something that is not acceptable, under any circumstances what-so-ever, is to chant about the holocaust, or extermination of a religion or race.

But onto the songs, and before we start, it's worth reminding ourselves of the following...

TEN THINGS THAT HAPPENED SINCE SPURS LAST TITLE WIN IN 1961

1. MAN WALKED ON THE MOON.
2. COLOUR TV IN HOUSEHOLDS.
3. THE KENNEDY ASSASSINATION.
4. BEATLEMANIA.
5. ENGLAND WON THE WORLD CUP.
6. ABOLITION OF CAPITAL PUNISHMENT IN THE UK.
7. OFFICIAL ABOLITION OF SLAVERY IN MISSISSIPPI.
8. THE FIRST EVER SUPERBOWL.
9. CASSIUS CLAY BECOMING MUHAMMED ALI.
10. THE BIRTH OF DANIEL LEVY

Here are some songs that celebrate over half a century of trying:

**"FOREVER IN OUR SHADOW YOU WILL BE,
YOUR HEARTS ARE FILLED WITH BITTER JEALOUSY,
TOTTENHAM, TOTTENHAM,
HAVE YOU EVER WON THE PREMIER LEAGUE?
HAVE YOU FUCK!"**
(Forever In Our Shadow by The Laughing Gooner)

This song emerged around the end of the first decade of the 21st century.

**"THERE IS A TEAM CALLED ARSENAL,
THE GREATEST OF THEM ALL,
AND WE WILL ALWAYS SUPPORT THEM,
WHETHER THEY RISE OR FALL, OR FALL,
AND WE'LL DRINK, DRINK, TOGETHER, IN PRAISE OF THE AFC!"**
(repeat twice)

WE'VE ONLY GOT ONE SONG

"FULHAM CAN STAY AT THE COTTAGE,
SOUTHAMPTON CAN STAY AT THE DELL,
AND AS FOR TOTTENHAM HOTSPUR,
THEY CAN GO TO HELL – TO HELL,
AND WE'LL DRINK, DRINK, TOGETHER, IN PRAISE OF THE AFC!"
(repeat twice)
(The Eton Boat Song)

Preferably sung with a boater whilst punting on the Cam! And by the way, Southampton didn't stay at the Dell they moved to St Marys in 2001. And speaking of the Saints:

**"YOU WON THE LEAGUE,
IN BLACK AND WHITE,
YOU WON THE LEAGUE IN BLACK AND WHITE,
YOU WON THE LEAGUE IN THE 60S,
YOU WON THE LEAGUE IN BLACK AND WHITE!"**
(When the Saints Go Marching In)

Another variation on this is "YOU WON THE LEAGUE ON PATHE NEWS". Pathe was one of the main broadcasters in pre colour TV football.

**"61, NEVER AGAIN,
61, NEVER AGAIN,
71, 2004,
71, 2004!"**
(Tom Hark by the Piranhas)

Spurs have won the league twice in their history. Arsenal have won the league twice at White Hart Lane.

**"WE WON THE LEAGUE,
AT WHITE HART LANE
WE WON THE LEAGUE AT WHITE HART LANE,
WE WON THE LEAGUE AT THE SHITHOLE,
WE WON THE LEAGUE AT WHITE HART LANE!"**
(When the Saints Go Marching In)

**"TO DARE IS TO DO, (Repeat once)
THIRTEEN LEAGUE TITLES,
YOU'VE ONLY ONE TWO!"**
(Sloop John B)

Round the middle tier of White Hart Lane there are hoardings with the intriguing, no irony intended, motto 'To Dare is to Do'. In 2015 a piss taking chant wasn't enough for the Arsenal away end who also felt the need to physically tear down the hoardings and cause a bit of media outrage.

VEGAS' STAG DO

**"HAVE YOU EVER SEEN TOTTENHAM WIN THE LEAGUE? (Repeat)
HAVE YOU EVER SEEN TOTTENHAM?
EVER SEEN TOTTENHAM?
EVER SEEN TOTTENHAM WIN THE LEAGUE?
HAVE YOU FUCK!"**
(Round the mountain)

Aimed at any Tottenham fan with no memory of the early 1960s.

"TOTTENHAM WATCHING EASTENDERS!"
(Go West)

In 2006 Arsenal played in the Champions League Final which may have clashed with the TV scheduling of the nation's favourite soap.

"WHAT YOU DOING SATURDAY?"
(Guide Me O Thou Great Jehovah)

A few days before the 1993 FA Cup final, Spurs came to Highbury and won 3-1. The away end acted like they had won a cup final – therefore needed to be reminded what plans they had for cup final weekend.

**"DONKEY WON THE DERBY,
LA LA LA, LA LA LA"**
(Let's all do the Conga)

To get to the 1993 FA Cup final, Tony Adams scored the winning goal against Spurs in the semi final at Wembley. And at the end of the tie, which was a replay of the disastrous 1991 semi final, the Arsenal end exclaimed:

"1-0... WE BEAT THE SCUM 1-0!"
(Blue Moon)

When Spurs outplayed Arsenal in the 1991 FA Cup semi-final, the chant "WE BEAT THE SCUM 3-1" was heard on a regular basis – up until the 1993 FA Cup semi-final when we beat the Scum 1-0.

"THEY'RE TURNING WHITE HART LANE INTO
A PUBLIC LAVATORY, (Repeat twice)
AND WE'LL ALL PISS UP AGAINST THE WALL,
STOREY, STOREY HALLELUJAH, (Repeat twice)
AND THE REDS GO MARCHING, ON ON ON!"
(Glory Glory Hallelujah)

The Hallelujah reference is to midfielder Peter Storey. Indeed, on Google maps a few years ago, White Hart Lane was turned into a public lavatory to prove the above 'prophecy' correct .

STOREY, STOREY HALLELUJAH, (Repeat Thrice)
AND THE SPURS GO MARCHING OUT OUT OUT!"
(Glory Glory Hallelujah)

Another shorter variant of this song was simply a celebration of Peter Storey allied to Spurs demise.

"WE ARE THE KINGS OF NORTH LONDON,
THE PRIDE OF THE SOUTH,
WE HATE THE TOTTENHAM,
CAUSE THEY ARE ALL MOUTH,
THE CANNON WILL FIRE,
THE COCKEREL FALLS,
WE ARE THE ARSENAL,
THE GREATEST OF ALL!"
(The Cock O' The North)

This song is a classic example of one that is regularly heard in pubs on match day, but not in the stadium. The fans that sing it in pubs are scattered and separated in the stands.

"IF I HAD THE WINGS OF A SPARROW,
IF I HAD THE ARSE OF A CROW,
I'D FLY OVER TOTTENHAM TOMORROW,
AND SHIT ON THOSE BASTARDS BELOW,

**SHIT ON, SHIT ON, I'D SHIT ON THOSE BASTARDS BELOW,
SHIT ON, SHIT ON, I'D SHIT ON THOSE BASTARDS BELOW!"**
(My Bonnie Lies Over the Ocean)

A 1960s staple, which should get a modern makeover.

**"A SPOON FULL OF SUGAR,
MAKES THE TOTTENHAM GO DOWN,
THE TOTTENHAM GO DOWN,
THE TOTTENHAM GO DOWN"**
(Spoon full of Sugar – Mary Poppins)

Alan Sugar was Spurs chairman between 1991 and 2001. Arsenal fans everywhere appreciated the work he did there.

**"DOUBLE, DOUBLE, DOUBLE,
SOL CAMPBELL HAS WON THE DOUBLE,
AND THE SCUM FROM THE LANE,
HAVE WON FUCK ALL AGAIN,
SOL CAMPBELL HAS WON THE DOUBLE!"**
(The Entertainer)

One season away from the Lane = two winners medals for Sol Campbell.

**"I DON'T KNOW BUT I'VE BEEN TOLD (one person)
I DON'T KNOW BUT I'VE BEEN TOLD (crowd)
CHARLIE'S BOOTS ARE MADE OF GOLD (one person)
CHARLIE'S BOOTS ARE MADE OF GOLD (crowd)
I DON'T KNOW BUT IT'S BEEN SAID (one person)
I DON'T KNOW BUT IT'S BEEN SAID (crowd)
HODDLE'S BOOTS ARE MADE OF LEAD (one person)
HODDLE'S BOOTS ARE MADE OF LEAD (crowd)"**
(US Army drill chant)

Very much in the style of a US army drill such as "Shout off"; a chant to be heard on the way to White Hart Lane in the 1980s when Charlie Nicholas and Glen Hoddle were the golden boys of North London football.

**"WHO PUT THE BALL IN TOTTENHAM'S NET?
CHARLIE, CHARLIE!
WHO PUT THE BALL IN TOTTENHAM'S NET?
CHARLIE NICHOLAS (Repeat twice)
WHO PUT THE BALL IN TOTTENHAM'S NET?
CHARLIE NICHOLAS!"**
(Camptown Races)

In the 1980s, Charlie Nicholas (1983-1987) was a goal scoring machine in the Scottish league and was a target of Liverpool; the dominant team of the decade in England. Instead, Charlie decided to live in the bright lights of London and chose to play for Arsenal.

The goals never flowed for him in the way that people had hoped for, but the Scotsman was always in the good books of the Arsenal crowd. Having a good scoring record against Tottenham helped that feeling towards him, as did his goals in the League cup final of 1987.

But after 54 goals in 184 games he was sold to Aberdeen by George Graham. Charlie returned to Highbury as a Celtic player for Paul Davis' testimonial match in July 1991. He was cheered and applauded despite scoring for Celtic in front of the North Bank. Also sang in the Paul Davies benefit game was "CHARLIE, CHARLIE, BORN IS THE KING OF HIGHBURY" in his honour following him throwing his shirt into the North Bank.

> "AWAY IN A MANGER,
> NO CRIB FOR A BED,
> THE LITTLE LORD JESUS STOOD UP, AND HE SAID:
> WE HATE TOTTENHAM,
> AND WE HATE TOTTENHAM,
> WE HATE TOTTENHAM,
> AND WE HATE TOTTENHAM,
> WE HATE TOTTENHAM,
> AND WE HATE TOTTENHAM,
> WE ARE THE TOTTENHAM, HATERS!"

Not exclusive to Arsenal. Other clubs have used this one as well against their local rivals– but an absolute cracker none the less.

"YOU'RE SO SHIT YOU MUST BE SPURS!"
(Guide me, O Thou Great Jehovah)

Sung at Spurs when things were going in our favour.

"ARE YOU TOTTENHAM IN DISGUISE?"
(Guide me, O Thou Great Jehovah)

Sung to anyone else who played like Tottenham.

> "HARK NOW HEAR,
> THE ARSENAL SING,
> THE TOTTENHAM RUN AWAY,
> AND WE SHALL FIGHT, FOREVER MORE,
> BECAUSE OF BOXING DAY"

(Mary's Boy Child)

It's staggering how many football chants are to the same tune as famous hymns and Carols. This one was made popular on the North Bank after boxing day home wins on and off the pitch in 1979 and again in 1983. This was a North Bank staple in the early 1980s.

**"YOU'LL ALWAYS BE SHIT, (Repeat once)
TOTTENHAM HOTSPUR,
YOU'LL ALWAYS BE SHIT!"
(Sloop John B)**

It's also staggering how many football chants come from the Beach Boys hit Sloop John B.

**"WHEN I WAS JUST A LITTLE BOY,
I ASKED MY MOTHER,
WHAT SHALL I BE?
SHALL I BE WEST HAM?
CHELSEA OR SPURS?
HERE'S WHAT SHE SAID TO ME,
WASH YOUR MOUTH OUT SON,
AND GET YOUR FATHER'S GUN,
AND SHOOT THE TOTTENHAM SCUM,
SHOOT THE TOTTENHAM SCUM!"
(Que Sera Sera)**

A good old wholesome 1950s song – corrupted by 1980s football fans.

**"CAN YOU HEAR US ON THE BOX (Repeat once)
TOTTENHAM ARE SHIT (Repeat once)
CAN YOU HEAR US ON THE BOX"
(Guide me, O Thou Great Jehovah)**

When television sets were in the shape of boxes, really weird things used to happen – such as live football matches being shown on terrestrial television to a huge viewing audience. On the occasions when Arsenal played on 'the box' they shared their views on Tottenham with the viewer. No surprise however, that 'CAN YOU HEAR US ON THE FLAT SCREEN LCD" never caught on.

**"WE HAD JOY, WE HAD FUN,
WE HAD TOTTENHAM ON THE RUN,
BUT THE JOY DIDN'T LAST,
'COS THE BASTARDS RAN TOO FAST!"
(Seasons in the Sun)**

This reworking of the Terry Jacks weepy is one of our favourite terrace chants due to its simplicity.

> "HELLO, HELLO, WE ARE THE ARSENAL BOYS, (Repeat once)
> AND IF YOU ARE A TOTTENHAM FAN,
> SURRENDER OR YOU DIE,
> 'COS WE ALL FOLLOW THE ARSENAL!"
> (Marching Through Georgia)

The Bromley Boys is a book about supporting Bromley FC (Mark's non league team) by Dave Roberts in the 1969/70 season. Within the pages he tells of his first visit in December 1969 to Arsenal with a Gunner friend.

"Despite being early we had to queue for 15 minutes to get into the famous North Bank, a vast expanse of concrete terracing where the home supporters stood. It was soon packed. As I turned round to survey the mass of bodies, a man towards the back raised his scarf and started to sing, his breath visible in the cold air. By the time he was a few words into the song, "HELLO, HELLO..." the whole North Bank seemed to have joined in. The noise was frightening yet electrifying too. Excitement was at fever pitch and the game hadn't even started yet. When Arsenal scored the whole of the North Bank surged forward like a tidal wave"

Despite not being an Arsenal fan he captures the essence of the time and the feel of the Highbury terraces. Often the tension and excitement was palpable and would build for ages before the game on the North Bank, and particularly on the Clock End if the game had attracted numbers of opposition fans.

1987

While we didn't realise it at the time, this year was probably the finest vintage for deriding our Tottenham neighbours. Or in modern parlance it was full of banter.

> "ONE-NIL DOWN, TWO-ONE UP,
> WE KNOCKED TOTTENHAM OUT THE CUP
> LA LA LA LA, LA LA LA, LA LA."
> (Give the Dog a Bone)

This song spawned a fanzine and commemorated an event which reinvigorated a club that had won nothing for eight seasons. After Charlie Nicholas' winning goals in the League Cup Final at Wembley, the team went from strength to strength under George Graham (manager 1986-1995).

In 1987 Arsenal and Spurs were drawn to meet one another in a League Cup semi final. Spurs won the first leg at Highbury 1-0 - and then at White Hart Lane, Arsenal won 2-1, after being a goal behind. Spurs won the toss for home advantage in the replay and in the second half took a 1-0 lead; not for the first time in the 1980s Spurs were on their way to Wembley – or so they thought.

A major factor in the Gunners' motivation for this classic 1987 comeback was a half-time announcement over the White Hart Lane PA; the presenter arrogantly stating how Tottenham fans could apply for their cup final tickets as we were 1-0 down. Up to this point in the decade, Spurs had the better record of the North London teams, with two FA Cup wins and a European triumph, whilst Arsenal had been generally mediocre and trophy less, despite some sterling early efforts in 1980.

Graham's up and coming team were in the process of changing the fortunes of the two clubs, and with eight minutes to go Ian Allinson (1983-1987) equalized in front of the Park Lane End. The away fans partisan spirit was let rip and fans were climbing on top of one another to let the home crowd know that the balance was shifting. George Graham was re-invigorating the club on the pitch, and the improving mood was spreading off the pitch amongst the fans.

These moments in the away end at White Hart Lane, are probably the ultimate contrast between the old culture of Arsenal fans compared to the modern day spectator fan. The energy, noise and tribalism were breath taking and ultimately entertaining, for both those participating and those just watching in the crowd.

Seconds remained of the 90 minutes and it looked like the game was set for half an hour of extra time, until David Rocastle knocked in a deflected cross under Ray Clemence - sparking utter delirium in the away end. Incredibly, this was the third time that season in which Arsenal had won 2-1 at White Hart Lane. In addition to the League Cup wins, we had beaten them 2-1 in January 1987 in the League.

As a euphoric bunch of Gooners left the ground they started singing in the streets of White Hart Lane after the League Cup semi-final win:

"SPURS WERE ON THEIR WAY TO WEMBLEY,
TOTTENHAM FUCKED IT UP AGAIN,
THE BOYS FROM TOTTENHAM,
THE ARSENAL STOPPED EM,
THE MUGS FROM WHITE HART LANE,
SHAME!"
(Spurs are on their way to Wembley – Chas and Dave)

Arsenal went on to win the League Cup Final 2-1 against Liverpool; once again after coming back from being 1-0 behind leading to a slight variation from the semi-final songs:

"1-0 DOWN,
2-1 UP,
THAT'S HOW ARSENAL WON THE CUP,
NA-NA-NA-NA, NA-NA-NA, NA-NA!"
(Give the Dog a Bone)

"1-0 DOWN,
2-1 UP,
WE FUCKED RUSHIES RECORD UP,
NA-NA-NA-NA, NA-NA-NA, NA-NA!"
(Give the Dog a Bone)

Meanwhile Spurs that year reached the FA Cup Final and faced little fancied Coventry; in the Wembley stands Spurs fans shrugged off the semi-final League Cup defeat by singing:

"THIS IS, THE PROPER CUP, ARSENAL!"
(We'll take more care of you - BT advert)

During the next North London Derby at White Hart Lane –which was a pre-season friendly in August 1987 (doubling as Chris Hughton's testimonial) Arsenal fans sung:

"YOU LOST, THE PROPER CUP, TOTTENHAM!"
(We'll take more care of you - BT advert)

As well as:

"WHEN GOUGH WENT UP,
TO LIFT THE FA CUP,
IT WAS GONE, IT WAS GONE!"
(In the Quarter Master's Store)

Tottenham captain Richard Gough and his side were expected to beat Coventry. Instead, a Gary Mabbut own goal was decisive and Coventry went up to lift the FA Cup. It soon became four 2-1 away scorelines within a year, when at the start of the 1987/88 season, Rocastle scored the equalising goal in another victory at White Hart Lane. ITV could not repeat Rocastle's goal because of technical issues caused by an industrial dispute, so Michael Thomas kindly did the job for them and a few minutes later scored a carbon copy of the same goal. Once again 2-1 after Spurs had taken the lead. This game was infamous for another reason - as of course it was the David Pleat match!

In the summer of 1987 the newspapers reported that David Pleat had been cautioned for kerb crawling twice while manager of Luton. The Sun ran another story, that while Tottenham manager he had been cautioned for a third time for the same offence. Allegations he denied.

The next fixture, after the original allegations, between the sides was on 18 October 1987. It was the weekend after the famous hurricane and Pleat was faced with a highly personal gale force from the Gooners:

"SEX CASE,
SEX CASE,
HANG-HIM,
HANG-HIM,
HANG-HIM!"

Aimed at any opponent who appeared in the News of the World or Sun the previous week, month or even year for perversions or "crimes" of a sexual nature. These could include a whole range of misdemeanour such as flashing or outrageous behaviour at a raucous party where too much flesh was revealed.

This chant rang around the Arsenal section for most of the match, and the song was accompanied by blow up dolls being thrown around at the Park Lane End. Coincidentally, on 23 October 1987, five days after the North London Derby, Pleat reportedly left his job for matters relating to his private life. Other chants were made up for Pleat, as unsurprisingly this matter was not forgotten.

"DAVID PLEAT, DAVID PLEAT, DAVID, DAVID PLEAT,
HE DRIVES A JAG AND FUCKS OLD SLAGS, DAVID, DAVID PLEAT!"
(Hooray Hooray it's a Holi-Holiday - Boney-M)

"DAVID PLEAT, DAVID PLEAT,
DRIVING DOWN THE LANE,
DAVID PLEAT, DAVID PLEAT,
ON THE PROWL AGAIN,

WHORES TO THE LEFT,
OLD BILL TO THE RIGHT,
KERBCRAWLER, KERBCRAWLER, KERBCRAWLER!"
(The Robin Hood song)

"SHE WORE, SHE WORE,
SHE WORE, FISHNET STOCKINGS,
SHE WORE, FISHNET STOCKINGS AND STILLETO HEELS.
AND WHEN I ASKED HER WHY SHE WORE THOSE STOCKINGS?
SHE SAID IT'S FOR HER CLIENT AND HIS NAME IS DAVID PLEAT,
DAVID PLEAT, DAVID PLEAT,
HE'S THE FAMOUS TOTTENHAM PERVERT AND HIS NAME IS DAVID PLEAT"
(She Wore)

And there's more!

"SHE'S A WHORE, (Repeat once)
SHE WEARS STILLETOS ON HER FEET,
AND SHE'S BEEN WITH DAVID PLEAT"
(Wembley, Wembley)

"DROP YOUR DRAWS AND THE FIVER'S YOURS,
DAVID, DAVID PLEAT"
(Wembley, Wembley)

So while the years 1971 and 2004 were spectacular, 1987 was utterly relentless throughout.

"STAND UP, IF YOU HATE TOTTENHAM!" (repeat)
(Go West)

Not a favourite for elderly or those with sports injuries. Sadly as Mark's creaking knees are dodgy, while the spirit is willing the legs can't manage this every few minutes. A much easier song to obey when we all stood up on the terraces anyway! This one tended to get the whole ground on their feet when sung at Upton Park as Arsenal and Hammers fans would always stand up in union regarding Tottenham.

ST TOTTERINGHAMS DAY

At home versus Aston Villa on 15 May 2016:- As the final game of the 2015-16 season showed, Ashburton Grove is capable of generating a tremendous atmosphere in the correct circumstances.

The crowd noise during a game is generally a reflection of what is going on the pitch, or in the wider circumstances, as the events at St James Park (Spurs eventually losing 5-1) kept the Arsenal match interesting. The one major exception to this is when a set of fans have designated a game as a special occasion and they have a sing-song and a laugh regardless of the game situation. In this game the Villa crowd all cheered Arsenal's goals and had a whale of a time too, despite watching their side getting hammered and being the worse team in the League by a long chalk. They added to the carnival atmosphere.

As news of the continued Spurs demise in the second half was picked up by the Arsenal crowd, a great roar, combined with laughter, was evident all-round the ground together with chants of:

**"WE'RE COMING FOR YOU,
WE'RE COMING FOR YOU,
TOTTENHAM HOTSPUR
WE'RE COMING FOR YOU!"**
(Sloop John B)

"STAND UP IF YOU HATE TOTTENHAM" - which had a massive uptake on the North Bank during this particular occasion, and rousing versions of: "YOU'LL ALWAYS BE SHIT, TOTTENHAM HOTSPUR, YOU'LL ALWAYS BE SHIT". "IT'S HAPPENED AGAIN...TOTTENHAM HOTSPUR...IT'S HAPPENED AGAIN" - Sung repeatedly and very, very loudly.

With the Gunners safe in beating Villa and the news of the 4th and 5th goals from St James' Park, the atmosphere went up a notch and was one of a party, and the best type – an unexpected one. Spurs had once again 'Spursed' it up, and allowed a quite frankly unlikely St Totteringham's Day to occur for the 21st consecutive year.

This time it looked certain to be cancelled, but never underestimate the gift that keeps on giving. Spurs had been the only true challenger to Leicester in their Cinderella season – and with two games to go were three points, and a vastly superior goal difference, clear of a lacklustre Arsenal team who had put in a feeble title challenge. Two defeats including the humiliating 5-1 thrashing at relegated Newcastle resulted in Spurs slipping into third place whilst Arsenal finished one place higher in second. On the North Bank end Darren Berry, author and well known Twitter spoofer, was seen engaged in starting yet another round of:

"IT'S HAPPENED AGAIN,
IT'S HAPPENED AGAIN,
TOTTENHAM HOTSPUR,
IT'S HAPPENED AGAIN!"
(Sloop John B)

A recent song used for the 2014 and 2015 FA Cup wins and the 5-2 victories in 2012, but is now forever associated with St Totteringham's Day.

"THE TOTTENHAM FUCKED IT UP, (Repeat once)
AND WE'RE ALL HAVING A PARTY, (Repeat twice)
THE TOTTENHAM FUCKED IT UP!"
(For he's a Jolly Good Fellow)

Yet another song that was heard later that evening.

Before 2016 the best St Totteringham's Day had been 'Lasagne-gate'.

"LASAGNE, WOO OO OO OH, (Repeat once)
IT GAVE TOTTENHAM THE SHITS,
WE LAUGHED OURSELVES TO BITS!"
(Volare – Dean Martin)

As documented in the discontinued book 'Spurs Fucked it up Again Volume 61': May 2006 – a Spurs win against West Ham at Upton Park would guarantee a finish in fourth place and qualification at our expense for the Champions League. Anything less, and Arsenal would finish fourth by beating Wigan in what would be the very last game played at Highbury.

Spurs lost 2-1 and Henry scored a hat trick in a 4-2 win; kissing the Highbury turf in an emotional goodbye to the old ground. It was then revealed that 10 out of the 17 man Tottenham squad, had a severe bout of food poisoning and blame was being firmly laid on the lasagne served at the Marriott Hotel in Canary Wharf. Conspiracy theories were rife: was the chef a Gooner? Was David Dein seen in the Canary Wharf area the night before the game? Was it actually the lasagne? Either way, the lasagne was awarded Arsenal Player of the Season for 2005/06.

**"IF YOU ALL HATE TOTTENHAM,
ALL HATE TOTTENHAM,
ALL HATE TOTTENHAM, CLAP YOUR HANDS!"**
(Coming Round the Mountain)

An old one that was always met with a massive round of applause.

"RAISE A BEER, IF YOU HATE TOTTENHAM!"
(Go West)

Or a latte for the new crowd.

"HAVE A DANCE, IF YOU HATE TOTTENHAM!"
(Go West)

Two post 1994 'Go West' chants sang in pubs and clubs

"LET'S ALL LAUGH AT TOTTENHAM, LA LA LA LA LA!"
(Let's all do the Conga)

**"THE WANKY TOTTENHAM HOTSPUR WENT TO ROME
TO SEE THE POPE, (Repeat twice)
AND THIS IS WHAT HE SAID - 'FUCK OFF!',
WHO'S THAT TEAM THEY CALL THE ARSENAL?
WHO'S THAT TEAM WE ALL ADORE?
WE'RE THE BOYS IN RED AND WHITE,
AND WE'RE FUCKING DYNAMITE,
ARSENAL ARE THE GREATEST FOOTBALL TEAM!"**
(John Brown's Body)

A timeless classic, based upon an American Civil War marching song circa 1860.

**"WHAT'S IT LIKE TO BE TOTTENHAM,
WHAT'S IT LIKE TO FEEL SMALL,
WE MIGHT HAVE LOST ON WEDNESDAY,
BUT YOU STILL WON FUCK ALL!"**
(What's It Like To Be Lonely)

At the end of the 2019 Champions League final the barman at the International Bar in Newtownards belted this out to disheartened Spurs fans frequenting the hostelry!

ARSENAL AGGRO HELLO HELLO

Arsenal's hooligan mob were known as the Herd, and like West Ham United (ICF), Birmingham City (Zulus) and Manchester City (The Guvners), they were known for being a multi-racial firm. The Arsenal mobs typically came from tough traditionally working class areas such as Camden, Hoxton, Finsbury Park, Holloway, Archway, Hackney, Burnt Oak and also many areas of South London. The Arsenal hooligan element in the South of the city were named SLAG: which stood for South London Army of Gooners.

The Herd have always maintained a policy of no publicity, especially in the form of films and books - which is one of the reasons why most fans, who were not involved in the hooligan scene, don't recognise Arsenal as having any sort of impact. One common perception is that Arsenal never had a credible mob. The Herd's counter to that perception is one of total indifference; those in the know – know about Arsenal – for those who don't - we couldn't care less.

In the early 1980s the Herd were asked to be in a TV documentary along with West Ham's ICF but they refused. The ICF documentary went on to become famous but The Herd cared little. All proposals for books get turned down and the chants in this chapter might be the nearest you'll get to reading about this culture at Arsenal.

Trouble at Arsenal, like football in general, began in the mid 1960s which went hand in hand and coincided with the increasingly boisterousness singing and chanting from the terraces.

Late 60s and very early 70s saw a respected and strong Arsenal crew, but this dissipated and by the mid 1970s other London clubs were bigger mobs, full of boot boys and skinheads and they would take 'liberties' at Arsenal. The kids who got bullied in the 1970s grew up and by the 1980s Arsenal again had one of the most formidable mobs in England; as the Herd's heyday was the 1980s and 1990s.

These kind of chants are now alien to the modern football ground, but between the mid 1960s and early 1990s, a normal occurrence on match day. At Arsenal, hooligan chants were just as likely to be heard in the Clock End where the home fans were within throwing distance of the away following. Though some were specific to Arsenal many of these chants were generic and sung by all team's firms during this period.

> "OOH-TO,
> OOH-TO-BE,
> OOH-TO-BE-A, GOONER!"
> (Chant)

The Arsenal lads got older, toughened up, and the tables got turned in the 1980s. Spurs used the word Gooner as a derogatory term for Gunners. Arsenal's hooligan mob, however, liked the term and were happy to be known as The Gooners. 'Ooh to be a Gooner' was initially a hooligan calling cry but today it's universal. All Arsenal fans are referred to as Gooners and this chant is mostly used by people who would never dream of throwing a punch at football, or indeed know of its origins.

> "B'JESUS SAID PADDY I SANG IT SO WELL,
> I THINK I'LL GET UP AND I'LL SING IT AGAIN,
> SO PADDY GOT UP AND HE SANG IT AGAIN,
> OVER AND OVER AND OVER AGAIN,
> B'JESUS SAID PADDY I SANG IT SO WELL,
> I THINK I'LL GET UP AND I'LL SING IT AGAIN,
> SO PADDY GOT UP AND HE SANG IT AGAIN,
> OVER AND OVER AND OVER AGAIN"
> (B'Jesus Said Paddy)

An Arsenal exclusive; no other set of fans sing 'Jesus Said Paddy' although it's very much associated with an old school set of supporters from past decades. Aside from 'Maybe It's Because I'm a Londoner', which was popular in the 1970s, this is rare in modern terms in that every other Arsenal song or chant is a variation; where here, no lyrics have been changed to suit football.

'B'Jesus Said Paddy' is an old Irish folk song that got adopted by Arsenal mainly because of the strong link of Irish players in the 1970s and 1980s. Not to mention Finsbury Park, at one time, being one of the most Irish populated areas of London.

> "EYES RIGHT,
> SKIN BACK TIGHT,
> BOLLOX TO THE FRONT,
> WE'RE THE BOYS,
> WHO MAKE MORE NOISE,
> WHEN WE'RE ON THE C*NT,
> WE'RE THE RIDERS OF THE NIGHT,
> AND WE'D RATHER FUCK THAN FIGHT,
> WE'RE THE GOONERS OF THE CLOCKEND, HIGHBURY!"
> (Eyes Right)

A Herd song inspired by a military chant. 'Bollocks to the front' means - those with the courage get to the front, which still gets an outing at Riders of the Night gigs.

LIAM BRADY
ARSENAL
1973-1980

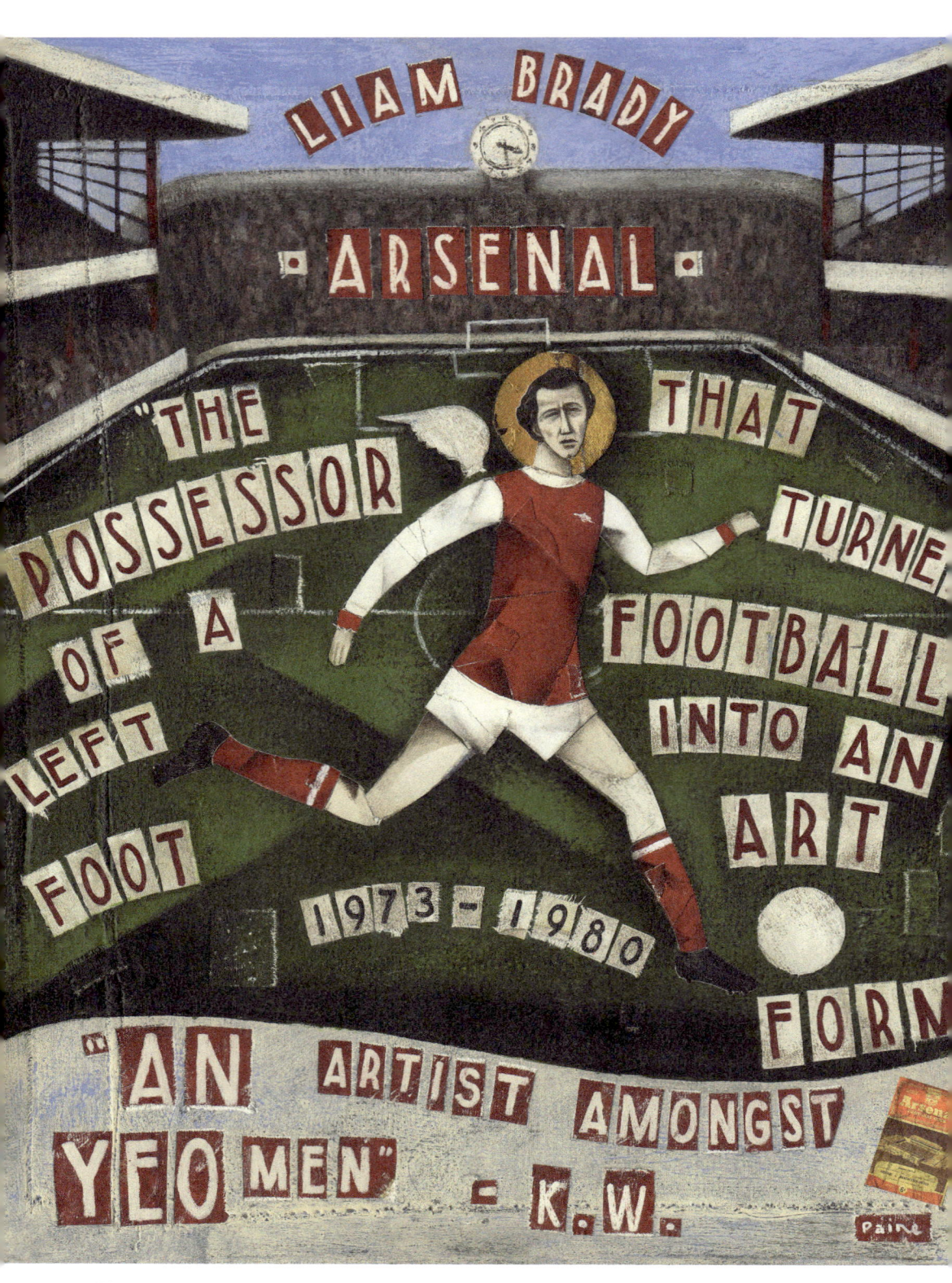

"The possessor of a left foot that turned football into an art form"

"An artist amongst yeomen" - K.W.

**"CLOCK END, CLOCK END,
DO YOUR JOB,
CLOCK END, CLOCK END,
DO YOUR JOB."**
(Chant)

Sung by the North Bank, pictured above, whenever the home fans in the Clock End got into scraps with the away support. "Clock End, Clock End, do your job..." was evidence of further interaction between the terraces. The North Bank would loudly and often request that the occupants of the Clock End carry out their "undefined" tasks against opponent fans.

**"WHEN IT RAINS, WE GET WET,
BUT WE AIN'T BEEN TAKEN YET,
LA LA LA LA LA LA LA LA LA!"**
(Give a Dog a Bone)

**"MY OLD MAN, SAID BE A TOTTENHAM FAN,
I SAID FUCK OFF BOLLOCKS YOU'RE A C*NT,
WE TOOK THE LANE IN HALF A MINUTE,
WE TOOK THE SHELF WITH TOTTENHAM IN IT,
WITH HATCHETS AND HAMMERS, STANLEY KNIVES AND
SPANNERS, WE SHOWED THE BASTARDS HOW TO FIGHT. "**
(My Old Man)

Based upon a Music Hall song popularised by Marie Lloyd in 1919, who incidentally was a girlfriend at one time of pre World War One Arsenal keeper Leigh Roose. The Shelf is a reference to taking Spurs' territory, it being part of their ground.

"WE LOVE TO GO A WANDERING,
TO SEE WHAT WE CAN WRECK,
AND IF WE FIND A TOTTENHAM FAN,
WE'LL WRING HIS FUCKING NECK!"
(The Happy Wanderer)

A 1960s-70s song that is taken from a 1954 chart hit, though with slightly more aggressive lyrics!

"FROM THE DARK, DARK ALLEYWAYS OF LIVERPOOL,
TO THE SHORES OF SICILY
AND THEY COME FROM HIGHBURY,
TO HELL WITH MAN UNITED,
TO HELL WITH MAN CITY,
WE WILL FIGHT, FIGHT, FIGHT FOR THE ARSENAL,
'TIL WE WIN THE FOOTBALL LEAGUE!"

"WE WILL FIGHT FIGHT FIGHT FOR THE ARSENAL,
TIL WE WIN THE FOOTBALL LEAGUE,
TO HELL WITH MAN CITY,
TO HELL WITH LIVERPOOL,
WE WILL FIGHT FIGHT FIGHT FOR THE ARSENAL,
'TIL WE WIN THE FOOTBALL LEAGUE!"
(The Halls of Montezuma)

Another 1960s-70s chant heard on the North Bank based upon an old US Marine marching song

"ON THE PITCH, ON THE PITCH, ON THE PITCH!"
(Stars and Stripes Forever)

At the infamous Villa game in May 1981, the North Bank sang this chant as they prepared to "help" Aston Villa fans in their championship revelry. There was to be no chant of "CLOCK END, CLOCK END DO YOUR JOB" as Villa had the whole of the Clock End - such was the potential importance of the match to their championship chances.
After the match, a mass invasion of both sets of supporters occurred on the Highbury pitch, primarily to "celebrate" Aston Villa's title win. The two sets of fans clashed as the police tried to keep order as best they could.

"YOU'RE GONNA TO GET YOUR FAAACKING 'EDS KICKED IN!"
(Chant)

Generally heard from the North Bank a few seconds after an opponent had scored, being aimed at their fans who had the temerity to celebrate the goal in the Clock End.

1994: THE HERD IN PARIS FOR THE ECWC SEMI-FINAL

"YOU'RE GOING HOME IN A LONDON AMBULANCE!"

"WE'LL SEE YOU ALL OUTSIDE!"
(Chant)

Both generic songs sung by all sets of fans on terraces all over the country, the ambulance service would be altered city by city, depending where you were.

"YOUR'E GOING HOME IN A COMBINE HARVESTER!"
(London Ambulance Chant)

Sung at Ipswich fans as a light hearted farm hand related alternative to the ambulance. And speaking of Ipswich, Matt recalls an incident at Portman Road at the start of the millennium which made him despise the way in which exuberant and passionate fans were treated by Stewards. In the dying seconds, Dennis Bergkamp had chipped the keeper and from the away fans viewpoint it looked-liked the ball was going in for an unexpected winner.

One fan in the front row literally jump out of his seat and over the hoardings which were a few yards in front of him. He quickly realised his excitement had taken him to the touchline area, so he quickly jumped back over a hording to his seat. Before you could shout 'Oh fuck it went wide', a mob of stewards jumped on him as if he was Lee Harvey Oswald holding a gun and John. F. Kennedy was strolling by. He was roughly dragged away and probably received a ban and possibly a court order as entering the pitch area is a criminal offence. No questions, no warnings, no understanding of a harmless mistake

"YOU'LL NEVER TAKE THE NORTH BANK!"
(Chant)

Sung, even though the North Bank had been taken on more than one occasion, possibly most completely in the FA cup quarter final of 1975 when West Ham beat Arsenal on the pitch and off it!

"WE WENT UP TO WOLVES TO TAKE THE NORTH BANK,
WE THEN WENT TO DERBY THEY WEREN'T WORTH A WANK,
SO TAKE MY ADVICE , THERE'S NOTHING SO NICE,
AS KICKING THE FUCK OUT OF CHELSEA!"
(Messing About on the River)

Other variations of this chant use Tottenham instead of Chelsea.

"COME ON WITHOUT,
COME ON WITHIN,
COME OUTSIDE AND GET YOUR HEAD KICKED IN!"
(Mighty Quinn)

Best stay inside then, as this was a more violent take on the Jim Furnell chant.

"I'M FOREVER BLOWING BUBBLES,
PRETTY BUBBLES IN THE AIR,
THEY RISE SO HIGH,
NEARLY REACH THE SKY,
BUT LIKE WEST HAM THEY FADE AND DIE,
TOTTENHAM ALWAYS RUNNING,
CHELSEA RUNNING TOO,
SO'S THE NORTH BANK HIGHBURY,
BUT RUNNING AFTER YOU!"
(Forever blowing bubbles)

In the 1980s, Arsenal and West Ham hooligan mobs had a serious rivalry. Serious enough for an Arsenal fan to be stabbed to death after game by the ICF. Things died down in the 1990s and although the two clubs still have a rivalry it's nowhere near as serious as it once was.

"WITH A BOW LEGGED CHICKEN,
AND A KNOCKED KNEED HEN,
WE AINT LOST A FIGHT SINCE I DON'T KNOW WHEN,
SO I WALK WITH A GIGGLE AND A WIGGLE AND A SWANK,
WE ARE THE ARSENAL - NORTH BANK!"
(Lord of the Dance)

That's quite nice for a hooligan chant.

"HIT HIM ON THE HEAD, (Repeat once)
HIT HIM ON THE HEAD, WITH A BASEBALL BAT,
OH YEAH, OH YEAH, OH YEAH!"
(Beat on the Brat by the Ramones)

That's more like it.

"AND TOTTENHAM CAME IN ONE BY ONE,
HURRAH HURRAH,
AND ONE BY ONE THEY ALL GOT DONE,
HURRAH HURRAH!"
(The Animals Came Marching In)

"THOSE WERE THE DAYS MY FRIEND,
WE TOOK THE STRETFORD END,
WE TOOK THE SHELF AND PAXTON WHITE HART LANE,
WE PICK ON WHO WE CHOOSE,
WE FIGHT AND NEVER LOSE,
THOSE WERE THE DAYS,
OH YES THOSE WERE THE DAYS!"
(Those Were The Days My Friend)

This Mary Hopkin's chart single was a number one chart topper in 1968 dating this to that period. The Herd were not invited to Top of The Pops to perform this hit.

"CHELSEA FC HAVE GOT A REPUTATION,
FOR SMASHING UP THE TRAINS,
UPON THE SOUTHERN REGION,
A HUNDRED ARSENAL,
SET A FUCKING AMBUSH,
TO KILL THE CHELSEA B'STARDS,
AND THE COPPERS TOO,
ONE-ARMED BABS, HE TRIED TO TAKE US ALONE,
BUT WE LEFT HIM LYING IN A POOL OF BLOOD,
AND LAUGHED ABOUT IT ALL THE WAY HOME!"
(Bonny and Clyde)

'One-armed Babs' was one of Chelsea's top lads in the early 1970s. Another variation on the chant started with: "ARSENAL FC HAVE GOT A REPUTATION, FOR CAUSING AGGRAVATION AT EUSTON STATION"

In the 1970s, 1980s, and to a lesser extent the 1990s, train stations such as Euston and King's Cross were where mobs would meet up to fight; leading to a question, if it could even be referred to as football violence, when instead it was youth gang violence.

> "HEIGH HO, HEIGH HO, TO TOTTENHAM WE WILL GO,
> WITH A BOTTLE AND A BRICK, AND A WALKING STICK,
> HEIGH HO, HEIGH HO, HEIGH HO, HEIGH HO,
> HEIGH HO, TO TOTTENHAM WE WILL GO,
> WITH A BUCKET AND SPADE AND A HAND GRENADE,
> HEIGH HO, HEIGH HO"
> (Heigh Ho It's Off To Work We Go)

After many arguments and debates, this version of Heigh Ho was cut from Snow White because the studio felt it 'inappropriate'. Six of the Dwarfs were known Gooners, apart from Dopey who had a season ticket at the Lane.

> "WHAT SHALL WE DO WITH THE TOTTENHAM BASTARDS?
> (Repeat twice)
> EARLY IN THE MORNING,
> STAB, STAB, STAB THE BASTARDS" (repeat once)
> (Drunken Sailor)

> "STANDING IN THE CORNER OF WHITE HART LANE,
> ALONG CAME A TOTTENHAM FAN WHO ASKED MY NAME,
> I PUT MY HAND IN ME GABARDINE COAT,
> PULLED OUT A RAZOR BLADE,
> AND CUT HIS FUCKING THROAT!"

These are a couple of the reasons why this book will not be available for purchase in the official club shops.

> "CHIM-CHIMNEY, CHIM-CHIMNEY,
> CHIM-CHIM-CHEROO,
> WE HATE THOSE BASTARDS IN CLARET AND BLUE!"
> (Mary Poppins)

Sung to West Ham. For the record, the scene in Mary Poppins where she stood on the Clock End and fought the ICF was removed from the final edit.

> "IF A SCOUSER NICKS YOUR COAT,
> PUT A RAZOR TO HIS THROAT
> SING AFC, AND CUT A SCOUSE TODAY,
> UNTIL THE SCOUSER GOES AWAY"

The faux cuddly reputation that Liverpool fans hold today wasn't held in the 1970s and 1980s for many away fans. Both Liverpool and Everton represented one of the most dangerous away days of the season and running battles in Stanley Park were nothing out of the ordinary. And for black away supporters it was particularly frightening, as the city of Liverpool represented one of the most racist away trips of the year.

> "WE TOOK THE SHED (Repeat once)
> EE AYE ADDIO WE TOOK THE SHED
> WE TOOK THE SHELF (Repeat once)
> EE AYE ADDIO WE TOOK THE SHELF
> WE TOOK THE HOLT (Repeat once)
> EE AYE ADDIO WE TOOK THE HOLT
> WE TOOK THE TRENT (Repeat once)
> EE AYE WE TOOK THE TRENT"
> (We've Won the Cup)

'We Won the Cup' or 'Ee Aye Addio' was a traditional chant from the 1960s. This corrupted version talks about the Shed at Chelsea, the Shelf at Spurs, the Holt at Aston Villa and the Trent at Nottingham.

> "TOTTENHAM FAN, HE IS DEAD,
> ESCALATOR ON HIS HEAD
> LA LA LA LA LA LA LA LA! "
> (Give a Dog a Bone)

After an early eighties altercation at the Seven Sisters tube station a Spurs fan died falling down an escalator.

> "RUN LEICESTER, RUN LEICESTER,
> RUN-RUN-RUN"
> (Run Rabbit Run)

This refers to a confrontation away to Leicester in early 1970s which was covered by the Daily Mirror along with pictures of Arsenal fans running through the streets. Leicester 's mob were known as the Baby Squad.

> "WE PAY FOR YOUR HATS, (Repeat once)
> WHAT A WASTE OF COUNCIL TAX,
> WE PAY FOR YOUR HATS!"
> (Sloop John B)

A more modern firm song; this one is usually aimed at the police whenever a large police presence was gathered round a pub, or were providing an unwanted escort.

> "WHEN I WAS A LITTLE BOY,
> MY GRANDMOTHER GAVE ME A CUTE LITTLE TOY,
> TOTTENHAM FAN HANGING ON A STRING,
> SHE TOLD ME TO KICK HIS FUCKING HEAD IN,
> KICK HIS HEAD IN (Repeat once)
> SHE TOLD ME TO KICK HIS FUCKING HEAD IN!"
> (My Ding a Ling – Chuck Berry)

Not sure we saw this one in Toy Story 3.

"COPPER DON'T BE A HERO, DON'T BE A FOOL WITH YOUR LIFE,
COPPER DON'T BE A HERO, YOU'LL GET YOUR HEAD KICKED IN"
(Billy Don't be a Hero - Paper Lace)

A self evident celebration of the police

"WE WENT DOWN THE LANE, UP FOR A FIGHT,
WE TOLD THE C*NTS, WE GOT A NEW IAN WRIGHT,
THEY SAID TO US, WHO CAN IT BE,
WE TOLD THE C*NTS, HIS NAME'S THIERRY HENRY"
(Tom Hark by The Piranhas)

"TO ALL YOU BASTARDS DRESSED IN BLUE,
THE CLOCK END HIGHBURY'S AFTER YOU,
AND IF YOU WANT TO TRY YOUR LUCK,
YOU WILL ALL GET KICKED TO FUCK,
FOR ALL YOU BASTARDS DRESSED IN BLUE,
THE CLOCK END HIGHBURY'S AFTER YOU"
(Oh Christmas Tree, Oh Christmas Tree)

Aimed at the Chelsea mob.

"WE ARE THE PARK,
THE FINSBURY PARK,
WE ARE THE PARK,
THE FINSBURY PARK"
(Chant)

Like most hooligan firms there were different factions in different parts of the city and the large Finsbury Park Arsenal mob, which was very multi racial, had their own chant.

"E.I.E"

Not so much a song or a chant but the war cry EIE would, from the mid to late 1980s, ring out whenever Arsenal's mob were confronting opposing mobs. There are at least three different views claiming its origins:
The first relates to 1980's steaming gangs who operated in London by rampaging through shops. Each gang had a 'warning chant' and EIE could have emanated from one of these gangs.
In the early 1970s at the Clock End, Arsenal would walk across the terrace from Avenell Road and mix in with away fans. They'd sing Old Macdonald had a farm, and as they reached the chorus the punches would be thrown EIEIO. By the later 1980s these chaps would reminisce about the good old days... Thirdly, during one away trip to Old Trafford, a Herdsman chewing on a pie or burger shouted 'Here They Are' on seeing a rival mob, and it came out EIE.

PROTESTS & CONTROVERSY

Most of the protests in recent years have centred around the ownership and management, most notably Stan Kroenke, Ivan Gazidis and Arsene Wenger. Wenger moved on in 2018, with mostly goodwill and respect; people remembering the great times more than the bad. Gazidis left the club on a whim in the same year. Kroenke however is like dry rot - not wanted but very hard to get rid of. Indeed, opposition about the American's running of the club seemed to have quietened down, not because anyone was satisfied with him, but because many felt their voices would be brushed aside. However, a multiple-fan led Twitter campaign #WeCareDoYou has seriously questioned Kroenke's custodianship of the club, gaining media coverage and support. It will be interesting to see how the protest evolves into the 2019/20 season, and if it can bring about a change.

Over two decades earlier, there were other areas of concern, not least the plans to put seats in the North Bank, and the consequent Bond scheme. A decade prior, there were the successful attempts to see the back of Terry Neill from the manager's role. Earlier still in the mid Sixties feelings towards Billy Wright went the same way. However, not all protest was inward looking and the finale of the 1990/91 season saw the whole fan base at one game telling the FA what they could do with their two points! So when someone says "it's not the Arsenal way" to protest, they are talking nonsense. But the fans only get exercised at major and obvious situations within the club that require resolution.

During the 2019 January transfer window, the club revealed there would be no funds available for new signings despite a squad that lacked quality, especially in defence as the likes of Mustafi were making Gus Caesar look like Franco Baresi. During the very same month, Stan's NFL team the LA Rams made it to the superbowl! One of the reasons the Rams had turned their fortunes around was because in American sports, failing teams get the first pick of the best young players in the draft which is why you don't tend to stay shit forever (with the exception of Cleveland Browns and New York Jets). Needless to say, our football doesn't work in the same way, and failing teams need serious investment or will fall behind. At the time of finishing this book, Arsenal seem lightyears away from challenging for the major honours. Hopefully in time we the fans will get proven wrong, but as it stands there is tremendous ill feeling towards the owner:

SING THE CHANTS YOU FUCKING TOURIST C*NTS

IT'S ARSENAL FC NOT A FUCKING MUSEUM

"GET OUT OF OUR CLUB, (Repeat once)
FUCK OFF STAN KROENKE,
GET OUT OF OUR CLUB!"
(Sloop John B)

Most notably sung at Everton in March 2016, at a time when Arsenal's title challenge had resembled a Tottenham title challenge, along with elimination from the FA Cup at home to Watford. 'Silent Stan' was disliked - perceived as greedy and tight - and during the previous two transfer windows only one outfield player had been bought; despite reports that the club had somewhere between £150 to £200 million in cash reserves. When a multi-billionaire is so tight that he won't even buy a decent wig, then questions need asking; followed by angry and venomous chanting.

Some blamed Wenger, others blamed Kroenke, some blamed both. Earlier in March 2016, Arsenal's rich owner with deep pockets had told press in America that "you don't buy a club to win titles" which for many Arsenal fans was the final straw before demanding a change of owner.

So, when the next protest came around late April 2016, versus Norwich, the messages were quite mixed. The organisers attempted to mute the quite vociferous 'Wenger Out' and 'Kroenke Out' and have a generic message of 'TIME FOR CHANGE: Arsenal is Stale - Fresh approach needed', which on the face of it, many could get behind, as it did not "disrespect" anyone but was asking for structural change.

However, on the day, most did not get involved as it took place during the team playing the game. Others decided it was just a dressed up 'Wenger Out' campaign and did not participate. The lack of focus - seats instead of standing, diluted any effort for like minded fans to sit together - was critical at the time in the stadium. Even so, the protest received massive sports media attention even featuring on Match of the Day so it did get its message over very well; if not entirely how the organisers had envisaged.

During this time, a very amusing sideshow was a large number of witty alternative flyers asking fans to hold them up with the 'Time for Change' signs. The Twitter image opposite, in particular, is relevant for this book:

"ONE ARSENE WENGER,
THERE'S ONLY ONE ARSENE WENGER,
ONE ARSENE WENGER!"
(Gauntanamera)

George Graham also had the same song. This chant for Wenger (1996-2018) was heard on a regular basis during the first ten years of his managerial reign. By the end of his second ten years it was very rarely heard in stadiums during the games. By that stage, large sections of the fanbase wanted a change – though Wenger loyalists, sometimes known as AKB's, still wanted him to remain as manager. The most significant time this chant was heard, post-2008, was during this Norwich match. The scheduled protest was short lived. The AKB's countered by singing Wenger's name via this chant and ultimately that strengthened his position as manager – much to the frustration of the fans who felt that one man had become too powerful and bigger than the club.

"WE WANT, WENGER OUT,
I SAY, WE WANT WENGER OUT!"
(Oops Upside Your Head)

Who would ever have thought it would have come to that? Over a decade earlier Wenger had capped a magical ten-year period by taking Arsenal to its first, and only, European Cup Final (Champions League). He was a hero, universally loved by the fanbase. In the second decade of the 21st Century the fanbase were divided in a horrible and toxic split. Some sick of the same mistakes and the lack of success, the other side loyal to Wenger no matter what. After an awful 2016/17 season opening loss at Ashburton - Boos and chants of "SPEND SOME FUCKING MONEY" were aimed at the manager. At the very next game in Leicester this was vociferously sung by many of the Arsenal travelling fans.

"WENGER GIVE IT UP, GIVE IT UP,
WENGER GIVE IT UP,
NANANANANANANANANANA,
WENGER GIVE IT UP, GIVE IT UP,
WENGER GIVE IT UP!"
(Baby give it up - KC and the Sunshine band)

"WHERE IS OUR MANAGER? WHERE IS OUR MANAGER?
WHERE IS OUR MANAGER? WHERE IS OUR MANAGER?"
(La Donna e Mobile – Verdi)

WE'VE ONLY GOT ONE SONG

Around about the time of the Bayern Munich 5-1 reverse in February 2017, and the fans were having groundhog day and deja vu, once again. Those in the Munich ground were also questioning the use of our manager's predilection to sit on his hands when the team were getting battered.

More aimless performances led to organisation within fans to set up a peaceful march as anti Wenger feeling had grown to boiling point and a protest march was organised. Because of the many wonderful memories Arsenal fans shared with Arsene Wenger in his first ten years at the club, fans felt they could never stage a Wenger Out protest - even though they wanted a change of manager and had done for many years. But the dam had broken. A few hundred people marched in March 2017 from outside the East Stand of the old stadium Highbury - to the new stadium and songs included:

**"ALEXIS IS RIGHT,
OUR MANAGER'S SHITE!"**
(Tom Hark by the Pirahnas)

In the first few months of 2017 it was obvious that Arsenal's star player Alexis Sanchez was disillusioned at the team's performances. His body language in games was one of utter frustration, and after a training ground bust up with his team mates, he was dropped to the subs bench in a 3-1 loss to Liverpool at Anfield.

In years gone by, the fans would probably have taken the side of the manager and his squad; on this occasion many sided with Sanchez as his frustration and ambition was shared with the fans. Sanchez seemed to represent what the club should be whilst most of the squad seemed to lack the same talent and winning attitude.

**"NO NEW CONTRACT,
NO NEW CONTRACT!"**
(Chant similar to USA..USA...USA...)

2017 and reports stated that a two year extension contract was already on the table for Wenger to sign, despite so much disappointment in the League and Europe since his last contract was signed three years earlier. The board wanted him to stay whilst the fans were bitterly divided. Fights in the stands between Arsenal fans had become normal, and the final years of Wenger's reign as manager were horrible for that reason alone. The division was miserable and Arsenal fans appeared to hate one another more than our traditional rivals.

**"WE WANT YOU TO GO, (Repeat once)
ARSENE WENGER, WE WANT YOU TO GO!"**
(Sloop John B)

**"YOU'RE KILLING OUR CLUB, (Repeat once)
ARSENE WENGER, YOU'RE KILLING OUR CLUB!"**
(Sloop John B)

Most of the fans on the march would, at one time, never have imagined that they would one day attend an anti-Wenger protest and sing chants asking him to leave the club. Gooner Oz said "It's sad that it came to this but he's been there way too long and the club is bigger than him. His tactics no longer work and we've been in decline since 2004. Not one credible title challenge in that whole time and his record in Europe is shocking, bar one good campaign in 2006. Someone else deserves a chance to either succeed or fail, it that really too much to ask for?"

After the march, the team lost 5-1 again to Bayern Munich. The 10-2 on aggregate score was by a very long way the Gunners' worst ever performance in their European history, and also the worst ever English team performance in the Champions League.

A second Wenger Out march a few days later had pretty much the same numbers, around 300-500 and similar chants.

However despite all the protests and general fan unrest, at the end of this season Arsenal won the FA Cup for a record 13 times, which made Wenger the most successful manager in the competition of all time. Three FA Cups in four seasons was an impressive achievement whatever side of the Wenger In or Out argument you sat.

"SPEND SOME FUCKING MONEY!"

Sack the Board! Arsenal v Aston Villa in 2011: the last home game of the season and fans vented their anger at the board for not spending money whilst at the same time increasing the already expensive ticket prices. Before the game, there had been a protest march from fans about the 6% rise in prices. The season had been the 6th in a row without a trophy - and after going 1-2 down to Aston Villa this chant transcended from the streets to the stadium.

"6%, YOU'RE HAVING A LAUGH! 6%, YOU'RE HAVING A LAUGH!"
(Tom Hark by the Piranhas)

Arsenal fans being frustrated at the club for being conservative with money was nothing new. The supporters and the board are a paradox; the fans as always were being asked to be extravagant spenders, whilst the club were tighter than a can of sardines.

**"WHAT THE FUCK DO YOU DO? (Repeat once)
IVAN GAZIDIS,
WHAT THE FUCK DO YOU DO?"**
(Sloop John B)

Sung during a protest march in December 2012, before a home game against Swansea City. The pressure group Black Scarf Movement mobilised around 1,500 fans to walk upon the stadium with the banner 'LET'S KICK GREED OUT OF FOOTBALL" as they demanded fairer ticket pricing for supporters.

WE'VE ONLY GOT ONE SONG

However, with the ever-increasing demands from players and their agents, clubs are often placed in a difficult position, though fans rarely get more than a cursory nod on this matter. The only time in living memory that fans have been able to unite was in getting the Category A surcharge for Season Ticket holders ceased against Barcelona in February 2016. As for Ivan Gazidis, he moved on to AC Milan in 2018, with many fans angry at him for allowing a culture of player contracts to wind down to the final year - resulting in the player leaving for a knock down price, or in the case of Aaron Ramsay, leaving on a free. Ian Wright was also critical of Gazidis as a chairman and along with expressing disappointment in his overall overseeing of the club added "When you look at the whole Suarez debacle, that was on his watch. A pound over the buy-out clause, for somebody that would have changed the direction of the club... I'm quite pleased that he's gone... that's not the kind of person that we need at Arsenal. We need someone who fights for the fans and gets us back up to where we need to be."

"CHOKE ON YOUR CAVIER!"
(La Donna e Mobile - Vedi)

During numerous ticket pricing protests at the Emirates stadium, this song has been aimed at the fans in the vast corporate areas.

**"WE LOVE ARSENAL, WE LOVE ARSENAL
YOU DON'T, YOU DON'T"**
(We're going to Wembley)

A chant aimed at the board and corporate fans during ticket price marches in the Emirates Stadium.

"WE'VE GOT MILL,
TWO HUNDRED MILL,
I JUST DON'T THINK YOU UNDERSTAND,
IT'S SITTING IN THE BANK,
BECAUSE ARSENE WENGER'S WANK,
WE'VE GOT TWO HUNDRED MILL!"
(Achy Breaky Heart)

In 2016, the winter transfer window once again was almost wholly ignored by the club, whilst many fans believed that Arsenal should have spent to give them a serious chance at the league, at a time when all the usual challengers had fallen apart and were behind us. They remained behind us, however, Leicester turned up and won the title on a points tally that was way lower than average for a Championship win.

"GEORGIE, GET THE CHEQUEBOOK OUT,
GEORGIE, GET THE CHEQUEBOOK OUT."
(Go West)

A chant not heard since the masses got used to online banking. When George Graham was manager and the team were underperforming you'd tend to hear the chant, generally at the end of his tenure.

"WE ALL AGREE,
LUKIC IS BETTER THAN SEAMEN!"
(Cielito Lindo, AKA the Ay, Ay, Ay, Ay song)

Yeah okay, we were wrong! John Lukic (1983-90 and 1996-2002) was a popular number one for Arsenal especially as he was between the sticks for the 1989 League triumph at Anfield. But at the end of the 1989/90 season, rumours were rife that George Graham wanted to sign David Seamen from QPR.

Fans disagreed with Graham's view that Seamen was the best goalkeeper in the country - and in the final games of the 1989/90 season, songs of support were heard for Lukic. It turned out that George knew. However, Lukic returned to Arsenal in 1996 as David Seaman's understudy but only played another 21 games in six seasons, meaning he made a total of 298 Gunners appearances.

"FIGHT, SING, WHEREVER YOU MAY BE,
WE ARE THE NORTH BANK HIGHBURY,
AND WE'LL GO DOWN IN HISTORY,
CAUSE WE ARE THE NORTH BANK HIGHBURY!"
(Lord of the Dance)

Sung part in anger, and part in reverence during the final few games of the old North Bank terrace at Highbury. The Taylor Report was making its mark on football culture and all-seater stadiums would soon be the law. The legendary terrace initially called, the Gillespie Road End, or the Laundry End, was to be replaced by a new seated stand and there were sit-down protests in the North Bank in efforts to try and reverse the decision to bulldoze the beloved terrace. An end that whole families had stood on, passing the baton from generation to generation, was to be replaced via a controversial bond scheme.

And at the end of the Saints game in 1992, around 3,000 fans stayed behind in a sit down protest and sung the sadly futile:

"WE'RE HERE TO SAVE THE NORTH BANK!"
(Same tune as 'The Referee's A Wanker")

Nobody wanted the North Bank to be knocked down, but the main objection was the club's method of paying for the new stand. At the beginning of the 1990s, both Arsenal and West Ham, paid for the new seated ends by offering fans cheaper ticket prices and ticketing priority, if they paid a four-figure lump sum up front. It went down badly from the supporters of both clubs who felt that this favoured fans with savings and was the beginning of a new era where the more affluent would be prioritised. Which it was! Football is now for the more affluent which is a normal and accepted fact, but back then people still believed that to be against the roots of the game. A few thousand actively protested, but that wasn't enough to force the board to change their minds. The beginning of the end was nigh for the people's game. If anyone asks when it was football changed – lead them to this point: compulsory seats!

"FUCK THE BOND, FUCK THE BOND, FUCK THE BOND!"
(Stars and Stripes Forever)

Whatever clubs did, they were bound by the Taylor Report, and each top outfit had to go all seating by a given period. The Bond protesters focussed anger towards the club Chairman.

"DAVID DEIN... IS A WANKER... IS A WANKER!"
(Hallelujah)

David Dein generally had a rosy image among Arsenal fans, but it wasn't always the case. During the bond controversy and his influential role in the formation of the Premier League, many fans in the early 1990s saw Dein in a very different light.

"CAN YOU HEAR THE MURAL SING?
I CAN'T HEAR A FUCKING THING!"
(Camptown Races)

'Highbury the Library' was born after the demolition of the North Bank terrace. From a fandom point of view, the 1992/93 season was a sad, empty season; though on the pitch we did win the domestic Cup double which was a major deal at the time. Where the North Bank terrace once housed a passionate fan base - there now stood a painted mural of fans. An all white, male set of fans at that; there were complaints that the mural featured no black or women fans, which for Arsenal certainly didn't reflect an accurate portrayal of the fan base. The spectator make up was duly altered on the mural but still the atmosphere in the ground withered. The Clock End which was still standing didn't fill the void. It felt weird – instead of the Clock End singing louder to compensate for the emptiness at the other end, everyone was just very confused!

Against Manchester City in September 1992 the club thought it would be a good idea to place speakers by the mural and blare out some pre-recorded chants in a bid to improve the atmosphere. Not the most glorious moment in Arsenal fandom, however, history does paint the mural in a different light - and a lot of people now agree that the mural provided better support for the team than the crowd in the West Stand Upper ever did. (Calm down - it's a joke ex-West Standers)

"WHO THE FUCKING HELL ARE YOU?" (Repeat multiple times)
(Guide me, O Thou Great Jehovah)

In the same game against Manchester City in 1992, there was more unwanted music from speakers. This was Sky Sports first ever game at Highbury and they bought with them fireworks – and the Shamen! 'Ebenezer Good' "E's are Good, E's are Good, He's Ebenezer Good" was a less than subtle glorification of a certain type of pill, and was a massive hit; being at number one in the charts for many weeks. Pop stars performing at half time was Sky's way of Americanising and changing the social demographic of football. The slogan was 'A whole new ball game'. The demographic in the Clock End at that time were still old-school football fans and weren't asking for a 'whole new ball game'. Many people liked football the way it was. Chants of abuse were levelled at the Shamen as they performed at halftime and as they walked off the pitch, they looked shaken and humiliated; this whole new ball game wasn't very friendly – not just yet.

"YOU'RE SHIT, AND YOU KNOW YOU ARE!" (Repeat multiple times)
(Go West)

Also sung at the Shamen from the Clock End.

**"YOU CAN STICK YOUR FUCKING TWO-POINTS UP YOUR ARSE, (Repeat twice)"
YOU CAN STICK YOUR FUCKING TWO-POINTS, (Repeat twice)
STICK YOUR FUCKING TWO-POINTS UP YOUR ARSE,
... SIDEWAYS!"**
(She'll be Coming Round the Mountain)

In 1990/91 George Graham's men were deducted two points by the FA as a result of a player 'brawl' [a bit of pushing and shoving] that 'marred' [made a good talking point] their game against Manchester United at Old Trafford. United were themselves deducted one point for their part in the fracas. The team and manager made it clear that they thought they could win the league anyway; which they did losing only one game all season and winning the league by seven points.

On Bank Holiday Monday 6 May 1991, Arsenal were gearing up to play Manchester United at home. A win would seal the title, however, it wasn't needed, as in the earlier kick-off second place Liverpool lost to Nottingham Forest. Arsenal were proclaimed champions for the tenth time, and reverberating around Holloway Road - and all roads in the vicinity of the ground was "YOU CAN STICK YOUR FUCKING TWO POINTS UP YOUR ARSE" which continued into the ground as Manchester United gave the Gunners players a guard of honour. Smudger hit a hat-trick as we cleaned up 3-1.

The song was a collective outpouring of relief - that the skirmish at Old Trafford and resulting two point deduction, didn't matter. Our boys had successfully seen off both North West rivals. It was also a typical Arsenal response to the other events that had transpired that season, such as Tony Adams being sent to prison for drink driving, which would have unnerved a less robust team.

Another angry chant was also heard that night:

"YOU'RE JUST A BUNCH OF WANKERS!"
(Chant)

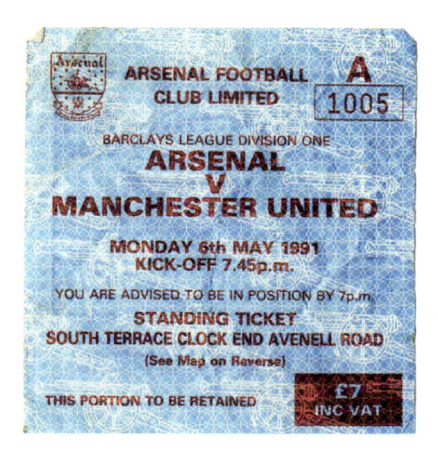

Sung by the North Bank to some of the Clock End. It was a night of celebration and after the win against Fergie's United, George Graham's team were set for a lap of honour as League Champions. A load speaker announcement warned that if there was a pitch invasion then the players would not be coming back out.

The Clock End didn't care and hundreds invaded the pitch in celebration, which back then was normal - and often expected. A few years earlier when Arsenal beat Everton in a League Cup semi Final thousands ran on to the pitch to which the commentator casually remarked "The crowd rushes onto the pitch" in an unassuming manner.

In May 1991, the well-behaved North Bank crowd wasn't impressed and chanted obscenities at the Clock End pitch invaders. In any case, the announcer was bluffing and the players did celebrate in front of the fans. By the way, look at the price of Mark's ticket in the picture which reads £7. Forward the clock just 25 years and the same game today would be around £75+ minimum.

**"STAND IN THE CLOCK END,
WE'RE GONNA STAND IN THE CLOCK END,
STAND IN THE CLOCK END!"**
(Guantanamera)

In 1995 Arsenal hosted French club Auxerre in the Quarter Final of the European Cup Winners Cup. The rain poured down and fans in the newly seated Clock End were in no mood to sit down in such weather. The whole end watched the game standing up and a wonderful atmosphere ensued. The stadium tannoy made repeated announcements, during the game, for the fans to sit down but was met with the same stubborn response.

"WRIGHT MUST GO, WRIGHT MUST GO!"
(Chant)

Billy Wright (1962-1966) made a good start to his managerial career, as in his first season, the club qualified for Europe for the first time in their history. However, by the 1965-66 season, poor results conspired to ensure Highbury was not a happy place.

"WE WANT A MANAGER!"
(Chant)

Wright was an English football icon as a player, but not as a manager. After the home loss versus Newcastle in March 1966, an angry crowd outside the

JOE BAKER SIGNS FOR NOTTINGHAM FOREST

marble halls were being held back by police as they vented their frustrations at Wright. These chants were heard from inside the stadium, as recounted in Peter Storey's entertaining autobiography "True Storey".

"BRING BACK, BRING BACK, BRING BACK JOE BAKER TO US!"
(My Bonnie)

Joe Baker (1962-1966) was sold by Wright to Nottingham Forest in February 1966. Since arriving at Arsenal he had scored 100 goals in 156 games and was regularly the club's leading scorer. In fact, his scoring feats at the time made him the eighth most prolific goals-per-game scorer in the Gunner's history. He has since been overtaken by Ian Wright, and currently sits in ninth place, one above Thierry Henry.

Not surprisingly the fans were somewhat disappointed at the loss of this highly talented and extremely popular forward. His transfer only added to the 'Wright Out' feeling among the support.

A week after the demonstration, Arsenal did not have a game, and consequently many Gunners fans went to see him at White Hart Lane where he influenced a 3-2 victory away victory for Forest. The Gunners horde at the Park Lane End; who were there to see Joe play and Spurs lose; treated him to the strains of "BRING BACK, BRING BACK, BRING BACK JOE BAKER TO US".

The fans began boycotting the remaining games and only 4,554 attended the game against Leeds on 5 May 1966. This was the lowest Highbury crowd for a first team competitive game in all the time spent at that fine stadium. The Last Post was sounded by a bugler on the North Bank, as Leeds ran rampant winning 3-0. Soon afterwards Billy Wright was gone, replaced by Bertie Mee.

"NEILL OUT! NEILL OUT!"

Historically, the club have rarely been prone to make snap decisions and remove managers on a whim, hence the club has not had a huge number of managers, especially when compared to other clubs. To use one example, Watford had nine managers in a six year period between 2013 and 2019. In contrast Arsenal had just five managers in the 36 year period between 1983 and 2019.

To highlight a rare, but not unknown, occasion of bitterness towards the boss, in 1983 the fans wanted Terry Neill to go. Neill (1976-1983) had turned Arsenal back into contenders and a specialist cup team in the 1970s and beginning of the 1980s. Not long into the 1980s however, Arsenal were declining, and after losing a home cup tie to Walsall in late November 1983 the fans had lost patience with Neill; who when he first came to Arsenal had to fight off the stigma of once managing Tottenham. At Spurs he couldn't shake off the stigma of once being an Arsenal player! He left Highbury in mid-December 1983 – and despite a disappointing and bitter end to his time as manager, Neill is remembered fondly, owing to the manner of the 1979 FA Cup final victory. He has regularly appeared as a guest on club history documentaries.

"WHAT THE FUCKING HELL IS THAT?"
(Guide me, O Thou Great Jehovah)

"WHAT A LOAD OF RUBBISH!"
(Chant)

In February 2002 the club proudly showed off their new crest. It was met with boos, derision and general opprobrium from the crowd as the crest was paraded at half time in the Southampton game at Highbury.

It was reportedly altered for copyright reasons, against the views of the majority of supporters and in the process lost a lot of the character and tradition of the predecessor. To say it was badly received by the fan-base is an understatement, and likewise it would not be an understatement to note that it is still badly perceived. Everyone loved the old crest - no one called for change. If the club had to change the badge for copyright purposes then what was stopping them from changing it to a beautiful and classy design – instead of one that looked like it had been drawn up by Gunnersaurus.

Aside from removing the 'Victoria Concordia Crescit' Latin motto, and having the cannon point the wrong way, it has all the appearance of a car badge and the class of a bubble gum wrapper; failing to invoke any apparent aspect of the history of the club.

It has been said that the marketing and design executives of the company used by Arsenal were threatened personally by many fans for fucking up our badge! A so called 'branding specialist' involved in the design change noted: "Over time it will be seen as much more exciting and much more dynamic than the current badge'. Well, it's been over fifteen years since the change and the current crest still looks more befitting to a Disney cartoon instead of a football club. Time alone cannot elevate something that was no good to begin with.

CONTROVERSY

**"IT SHOULD HAVE BEEN YOU, (repeat once)
SHOT IN ANGOLA,
IT SHOULD HAVE BEEN YOU!"**
(Sloop John B)

A chant directed at Emanuel Adebayor (2006-2009) who after signing for Arsenal scored a lot of goals in his second season, had a public pay dispute with the club, fell out with the fans, and left for Manchester City. In his first game against his old club, he scored in a 4-2 win for City and overtly taunted the Arsenal fans in the away end; who in turn went ballistic.

Signing for Tottenham in 2011 did wonders for his un-popularity among Gooners and he even became as disliked (well nearly) as Teddy Sheringham. Adebayor competed for Togo in the African Nations Cup in 2010 which was marred by a gun attack on the Togo team bus by a fringe terrorist group. Three people on the team bus were killed.

"SADDAM RUNS FROM ARSENAL!"
(Let's all do The Conga)

Arsenal played Everton in January 1991 a few days after the start of the first Gulf War. A 1-0 win assisted the team in their quest for the title, as the North Bank affirmed their disdain for Iraq's leader.

**"HE'S TWITCHING AGAIN, (repeat once)
HARRY REDKNAPP,
HE'S TWITCHING AGAIN!"**
(Sloop John B)

One of a number of twitch songs sung at Harry Redknap which became a focus of complaint from the former Spurs manager.

**"HE EATS WITH HIS FEET, (Repeat once)
GARETH BALE... HE EATS WITH HIS FEET!"**
(Sloop John B)

1970s and 1980s football was on too many disgusting occasions, marred by monkey chanting and overt racism towards black players. Thankfully, in this country at least, significant progress has been made to ensure this is never repeated. However, one strange incident against Tottenham, begs the question... is it racist for a white man to throw a banana at another white man? This above chant, aimed at Gareth Bale, didn't appear that controversial, however, an incident related to the chant did get one fan in serious trouble when he threw a banana at Bale at White Hart Lane and got himself a fine and a ban.

"SHE SAID YES GIROUD, SHE SAID YES."
(Kumbaya)

Not controversial but related to the Van Persie chant, which we decided not to print here as it directly references rape allegations. Giroud made headlines for allegedly sleeping with a girl the night/morning before Arsenal had an early kick off the next day. On the match day, Liverpool smashed us 5-1 and Giroud had a stinker.

"GO AND DO THE WASHING UP!"
(Guide me, O Thou Great Jehovah)

Unfortunately sung to Arsenal's Ladies team by the old North Bank terrace as they did a lap of honour.

"GET YOUR TITS OUT FOR THE LADS!"
(Guide me, O Thou Great Redeemer)

In the 1980s, the 'Make Money With Arsenal' ladies patrolled pitch-side in their red outfits selling lottery tickets at half time and often had to endure these loud bovine requests. Juxtapose these chants against the very warm and respectful reaction the Arsenal ladies got at half time of the last game in 2015/16 on parading their 14th WFA trophy which had been won the day before. Times change, and in this case much for the better.

"WHAT DO YOU THINK OF TOTTENHAM? (one person)
SHIT (wider crowd)
WHAT DO YOU THINK OF SHIT? (one person)
TOTTENHAM (wider crowd)
THANK YOU (one person)
THAT'S ALRIGHT ... (wider crowd)
WE HATE TOTTENHAM AND WE HATE TOTTENHAM,
WE HATE TOTTENHAM AND WE HATE TOTTENHAM,
WE HATE TOTTENHAM AND WE HATE TOTTENHAM,
WE ARE THE TOTTENHAM HATERS!"
(Chant)

A chant Jack Wilshere (2001-18) once used; sorry twice used, during Arsenal's FA Cup Winners parades in 2014 and 2015. Disappointed that he wasn't fined by the FA the first time around, he made sure he got the microphone out and repeated it in 2015; whilst wearing a pair of shades and sunhat and looking more suited to the Glastonbury festival than a football team parade. The fans loved it and were happy and willing participants. What everyone didn't see was Arsene Wenger starting a rendition of 'FUCK OFF YOU SPURS". Unfortunately, crowd favourite Wilshire, did not live up to his obvious potential, as injuries curtailed his appearances to 197 games.

WE'VE ONLY GOT ONE SONG

**"POSH SPICE IS A SLAPPER,
SHE WEARS A WONDERBRA,
AND WHEN SHE'S SHAGGING BECKHAM,
SHE THINKS OF RAY PARLOUR!"**
(My Old Man's a Dustman)

Neither Posh Spice or Ray Parlour have every confirmed, or denied, this unfounded load of old tosh!

**"MURDERERS, MURDERERS, MURDERERS,
MURDERERS, MURDERERS, MURDERERS,"**
(Chant)

Referencing a very dark era for the game, if ever a chant touched a raw nerve it was this one. Arsenal fans at Anfield sung 'Murderers' in what was the first competitive game at Anfield since the Heysel Disaster in 1985, when crowd trouble resulted in a wall collapsing and crushing 39 Juventus supporters to death.

It was also sung in December of that year in the first home game that Gooners were able to voice their disgust at Liverpool fans over the Heysel tragedy. Seemingly, being seen to be single-handedly responsible for getting all English teams banned from European competition only added to the feeling.

"CHELSEA RENT BOY, CHELSEA RENT BOY... HELLO, HELLO!"
(Chant)

During the 1980s and 1990s when this chant was common, it wasn't that controversial. In recent years however, fans who have used this song have come under fire for its homophobic overtones, and consequently it is now moribund.

"YOU WISH, YOU WERE ENGLISH!"
(Go West)

Sung at Cardiff in 2010. At the time of writing, this was the last time Arsenal fans were able to stand on a large open terrace in a competitive game (we are not including the Sutton tie in 2017 as it wasn't a large terrace). Arsenal were drawn against the Bluebirds in the FA Cup third round which was Cardiff's last season of playing home games at Ninian Park. Cardiff fans responded to this chant by singing the same chant back to Arsenal fans, which was either in relation to Arsenal's ethnic diversity of support – or the lack of home-grown players that represented the club.

GREAT COMEBACKS & CELEBRATIONS

Arsenal fans have a long history of terrace exchanges as very early evidence came, only five years after the club was formed, in the London Senior Cup semi-final versus Clapton in February 1891 where there was witty repartee between the two sets of supporters. This was the biggest competition in the South at the time and both sides had a fair sprinkling of supporters around the Kennington Oval. The very same location that now houses Surrey CCC and the England Cricket team.

The fans exchanged friendly banter; the Claptonites reminding their Arsenal counterparts of Clapton's early season victory over the Reds. In riposte, the Arsenal crowd reminded their adversaries of recent defeats Clapton had suffered at the hands of Nottingham Forest and Casuals.

Fairly obviously the celebrations are mainly linked to actually winning something, such as the League or FA cup, though in the main - these are mostly generic amongst all sets of fans whose teams win trophies.

GREAT COMEBACKS

"ARSHAVIN SCORED, (Repeat once)
HOW SHIT MUST YOU BE?
ARSHAVIN SCORED!"
(Sloop John B)

Sung during a League cup tie in September 2012, in response to Coventry fans singing "HOW SHIT MUST YOU BE, IT'S ONLY 2-0." Andrey Arshavin (2009-2013) scored the third goal in a 6-1 victory in which most of the first team were rested.

The song was a sad reflection on how far Arshavin's reputation had swung - from being the most dangerous and influential player in the team – into a squad player who was regarded as unmotivated. Indeed, this game was one of only two matches he started, in this, his final season for the club (the other being the bizarre 7-5 win at Reading in the same competition).

When he signed in the winter window of 2009 it was off the back of a great performance in Euro 08 which made him one the most sought after players in Europe. In Arshavin's first two seasons he enforced that reputation – most notably in a 4-4 draw at Anfield in which he scored all four goals.

His form began to dip, and soon Arsenal were looking to offload him to anyone – as opposed to fending off other big clubs from a prized asset. In this game against Coventry in 2012 he had just returned from a loan spell at Zenit St. Petersburg where he would soon join in a no fee deal in 2013.

"WE'VE ONLY WON IT TEN TIMES!"
(Blue Moon)

Blackburn fans were under the impression that football started in 1992 when the Premier League was formed. Hence the chant to Arsenal fans in 1997-98 of "HAVE YOU EVER WON THE PREMIER LEAGUE".

Arsenal responded with the reminder that we are one of only three clubs who have won the league in double figures. Indeed, Arsenal in 1971, became the first club to win the league as many as eight times. Blackburn won that afternoon in 1997 and Arsenal were written off as title contenders. The team responded well and by May won the league for the first time - since 1991.

"SHALL WE WIN THE LEAGUE FOR YOU?"
(Guide me, Thou, O Great Jehovah)

Sung to Manchester City fans in response to "SHALL WE SING A SONG FOR YOU". In the first years of the 21st Century Arsenal were consistently battling for the title against City's bitter rivals Manchester United.

"SIT DOWN YOU PAEDOPHILES!"
(La Donna e Mobile - Verdi)

For years Spurs fans sung 'SIT DOWN YOU PAEDOPHILE' to Arsene Wenger due to allegations based on quite literally - nothing.

"YOU'RE NOT RINGING ANYMORE!"
(Guide me, Thou, O Great Jehovah)

Near the start of the 2003/04 season, Arsenal entertained newly promoted Portsmouth at Highbury. Pompey fan John Anthony Portsmouth Football Club Westwood (yes that is his name) became a recognisable face by going to games looking like a blue and white version of a tattooed Screaming Lord Sutch. His trademark show of support was to ring a bell throughout the game, generally to the Pompey Chimes tune.

But at Highbury in September 2003 the killjoy stewards decided to chuck him out for persistent standing. Matt was a few rows away and felt disgusted at the new draconian attitude that had crept into the game – however every cloud has a silver lining and what followed was perhaps the best chant ever.

Incidentally John APFC Westwood is an Antiquarian bookseller from Petersfield in Hampshire

"BORING, BORING, ARSENAL!"

Regularly sung back at the football world as a whole. Normal to hear when the opposition is on the end of a whooping.

**"TOTTENHAM MIND THE GAP,
TOTTENHAM, TOTTENHAM,
MIND THE GAP…"**

In the final third of the 2011/2012 season, Spurs had built a lead over Arsenal and the message coming from the Lilywhite side of North London was 'Mind The Gap'. Just to emphasise the message fully, and rub our noises in it, T-Shirts were produced that had 'Mind The Gap' displayed on a London Underground symbol.

In February 2012, Spurs were ten points clear of Arsenal and came to the Emirates determined to extend the gap further. They took an early 2-0 lead, but then the whole season changed: Sagna and Van Persie scored to make it 2-2 and Walcott was the star of the second half as he scored two goals in a 5-2 win. The gap had been reduced to seven points and as the season came to a close – Arsenal fans had a message for Tottenham: Mind the Gap.

Spurs finished one place below Arsenal in fourth place; normally enough to secure a Champions League spot. However, in a cruel yet amusing twist, Chelsea who finished fifth, won the Champions League, claiming the remaining English Champions League spot for the following season. As for the T-shirts – they sold out. Gooners went on the Spurs fan website and bought them whilst stocks lasted. The following season in 2012/13, five things happened that bought a feeling of De ja vu: Spurs built up a healthy lead over Arsenal by the final third of the season; 'Mind the Gap' slogans started appearing at N17; Arsenal beat Spurs 5-2 at home, November 2012; Spurs bottled it in March; Arsenal fans sung 'Mind the Gap' in May.

**"HE'S WON MORE THAN YOU, (Repeat once)
AARON RAMSEY,
HE'S WON MORE THAN YOU!"
(Sloop John B)**

This chant was heard in January 2016 and was in response to one of the most bovine chants of all time. In 2010 Ramsey had his leg broken by Stoke's Ryan Shawcroft after a clumsy tackle by the defender. Stoke fans were angry at Ramsey and booed him for having the audacity to have his leg broken and making their club look bad.

To Sloop John B (what else) they chanted that Ramsey would never walk again – whilst Ramsey was on the pitch - having the previous two seasons won the FA Cup and scoring the winning goal in the 2014 final. The next season after this reposte was heard, he did something unique, namely score another FA Cup winner, making him the only player to have scored two winners in different FA Cup finals in the history of modern English football. The sad Stoke chant was a bit like screaming 'YOU'LL NEVER GET LAID AGAIN' to Mick Jagger, George Best or Frank Worthington outside their dressing rooms in the 1960 and 1970s. As for Ramsey he left Arsenal at the end of the 2018/19 season, after 11 years, 369 games and 64 goals for the Gunners – signing on reported astronomical wages for Italian Giants Juventus.

> "YOU ARE WANKERS, (Repeat three times)
> FROM THE LANE,
> YOU ARE WANKERS, (Repeat three times)
> FROM THE LANE!"
> (We Are Sailing – Rod Stewart)

This always used to follow the droning Spurs fan's chant: "WE ARE TOTTENHAM FROM THE LANE". Not commonly heard beyond the 1990s, for no obvious reason because the song is still as true as it was in the past. Maybe even truer.

> "I'M FOREVER BLOWING BUBBLES, PRETTY BUBBLES IN THE AIR,
> THEY FLY SO HIGH , THEY REACH THE SKY,
> THEY'RE LIKE WEST HAM, THEY FADE AND DIE!"
> (Blowing Bubbles)

The best comeback to 'Blowing Bubbles' was when the Clock End sung the regular version – but in ludicrously high pitched voices. This occurred in September 1997 sending the Hammers fans crazy and some coins were thrown in response. Of course the 4-0 score line didn't help matters either.

> "IF LEE DIXON PLAYS FOR ENGLAND SO CAN I"
> (She'll be coming round the mountain)

After his wonder own goal early on against Coventry in September 1991 at Highbury, the away fans started singing this popular refrain. Not to be outdone the North Bank joined in too!

CELEBRATIONS

> "ALL THINGS BRIGHT AND BEAUTUFUL,
> ALL CREATURES GREAT AND SMALL,
> ARSENAL WON THE FOOTBALL LEAGUE,
> AND TOTTENHAM WON FUCK ALL!"
> (All Things Bright and Beautiful)

Another church hymn corrupted by football fans.

**"LET'S GO FUCKING MENTAL, (Repeat once)
LA LA LA LA!" (Repeat once)**
(Let's all do the Conga)

This one died in the stadiums when the terraces went. However, it did survive in some of the pubs and bars. The whole chant relies upon on a whole group of people together who want to jump around and go ballistic - and generally that's not going to happen in seated stadiums in the Premier League. This was a common celebration and chant in the terraces at Highbury if the team were winning and playing well.

When people discuss atmosphere it's always volume related. What doesn't get recognised is how static the crowd now is. The movement and energy of the supporters was always just as important as noise. How ballistic you went when a goal was scored was not dependant on how big or important the game was; it's just what you did. What was particularly breath taking was the sight of the away goal celebrations at Highbury. Although every away goal was gutting – the sight of fans going mental on an away terrace was mesmerising as well as annoying. The energy and movement was wild, and for those who don't remember, the best comparison is to simply watch clips of 1980s and 1990s football - and analyse the nature of the goal celebrations.

"WE ARE THE CHAMPIONS!"(clap, clap, clap, clap, clap)
(We are the Champions)

Heard during the 1971 FA Cup final. This was not the Queen version for which we would have to wait another six years before Freddie belted it out. This was the same chant that was later utilised as the theme for the popular 1970's children's TV programme also called "We are the Champions".

"WE ARE UNBEATABLE!" (Repeat multiple times)
(La Donna e Mobile)

The Invincible chant - 2004.

**"49, 49, UNDEFEATED,
49, 49, I SAY,
49, 49, UNDEFEATED
PLAYING FOOTBALL THE ARSENAL WAY!"**
(Hymn: Oil in my lamp)

A rehash of the Manchester United '20 Times' song, it was penned almost a decade after the feat and regularly gets sung at matches.

**"WE'RE ON OUR WAY,
WE'RE ON OUR WAY,
WE'RE GOING TO WEMBLEY,
WE'RE ON OUR WAY,**

HOW WE GET THERE, WE DON'T KNOW,
HOW WE GET THERE, WE DON'T CARE,
ALL I KNOW IS WE ARE ON OUR WAY..." (repeat)

Originally a Sunderland ditty, which they sang in the 1992 Cup final. The Black Cats fans singing "WE ARE SUN-DER-LAND" rather than "WE'RE GOING TO WEM-BER-LEY'. Similarly, the Arsenal fans, for the 2006 Champions League Final, replaced the word 'Wembley' with 'Paris'. It also gets altered especially for European games, such a Baku, or special away matches. This song was first sung by Gunners at the Millennium Stadium where the word Cardiff replaced Wembley at the 2001 FA Cup final against Liverpool. This was the first peacetime FA Cup final away from Wembley since 1923. Arsenal lost a one sided cup final 2-1; one sided for the losers that is, Liverpool got hammered for most of the game but won with two late Michael Owen goals (and an unaccountably unseen handball in the first half).

This chant is also the introduction for the Riders of the Night 2015 Unofficial FA Cup final song. However bearing in mind its pedigree, it is a wonder it is ever sung - or indeed why we placed it in the celebrations section!

"WE ARE TOP OF THE LEAGUE,
SAY WE ARE TOP OF THE LEAGUE!"
(Oops Upside Your Head)

Sung in the times that we are top of the League

"WE'LL BE TOP AT FIVE O'CLOCK!"
(Guide me, O Thou Great Jehovah)

Heard when most matches were played at 3:00 on a Saturday whenever we were top of the league.

"WE SHALL NOT, WE SHALL NOT BE MOVED,
WE SHALL NOT, WE SHALL NOT BE MOVED,
JUST LIKE THE TEAM THAT'S GONNA WIN THE FA CUP,
WE SHALL NOT BE MOVED!"

Generally chanted near the end of a cup tie close to the end rounds of the competition. It can also be used to serenade the Football League winners.

"WE'RE GONNA WIN THE LEAGUE, (Repeat once)
AND NOW YOU'RE GONNA BELIEVE US, (Repeat once)
WE'RE GONNA WIN THE LEAGUE!"
(For he's a Jolly Good Fellow)

A 1991 favourite, amongst other years.

"WE WON THE CUP, WE WON THE CUP,
EE AYE ADDIO, WE WON THE CUP!"
(Ee Aye Addio)

A self-explanatory song, which was not overly sung very often in the 1960s at Highbury; the only trophy less decade from the 1930s to now. But this chant got used properly in the 1970s.

"WHEN TONE GOES UP,
TO LIFT THE FA CUP,
WE'LL BE THERE, WE'LL BE THERE!"
(In the Quarter Master's Store)

Sung in 1993 by those lucky enough to get tickets for the FA Cup Final between Arsenal and Sheffield Wednesday. Tony Adams did lift the FA Cup and many fans, who did not expect to witness the tie live, were there because it went to a replay and more tickets were available to fans of the competing clubs, than had been for the first game which ended 1-1.

Tickets went on general sale for as little as £10 and Arsenal won 2-1 with a last minute goal from Andy Linighan. This was the last ever time that the FA Cup Final went to a replay as new laws were on their way, resulting in future finals being settled in penalty shoot-outs.

"2-0, AND YOU FUCKED IT UP!" (repeat as required).
(Go West)

A chant sung to Hull City support whenever we have played the Tigers since the FA Cup 2014 final. This was heard in February 2016 during the FA Cup Fifth round tie which was drawn, and then a short while later in the replay which we won 4-0. Obviously it is a generic chant for any club who let any lead slip away.

"DRINK, DRINK, WHEREVER YOU MAY BE,
WE ARE THE DRUNK AND DISORDERLY,
BUT WE DON'T GIVE A SHIT, AND WE DON'T A FUCK,
COS WE CAME HOME WITH THE CUP WINNERS' CUP!"
(Lord of the Dance)

"WHEN WE WENT TO EUROPE,
THEY DIDN'T GIVE US A CHANCE,
WE DONE 'EM IN TORINO,
WE KICKED THEIR ARSE IN FRANCE,
WE WENT TO COPENHAGEN,
WE HAD A FUCKING BALL,
ARSENAL WON THE CUP WINNERS' CUP,
AND TOTTENHAM WON FUCK ALL!"
(The Laughing Policeman)

WE'VE ONLY GOT ONE SONG

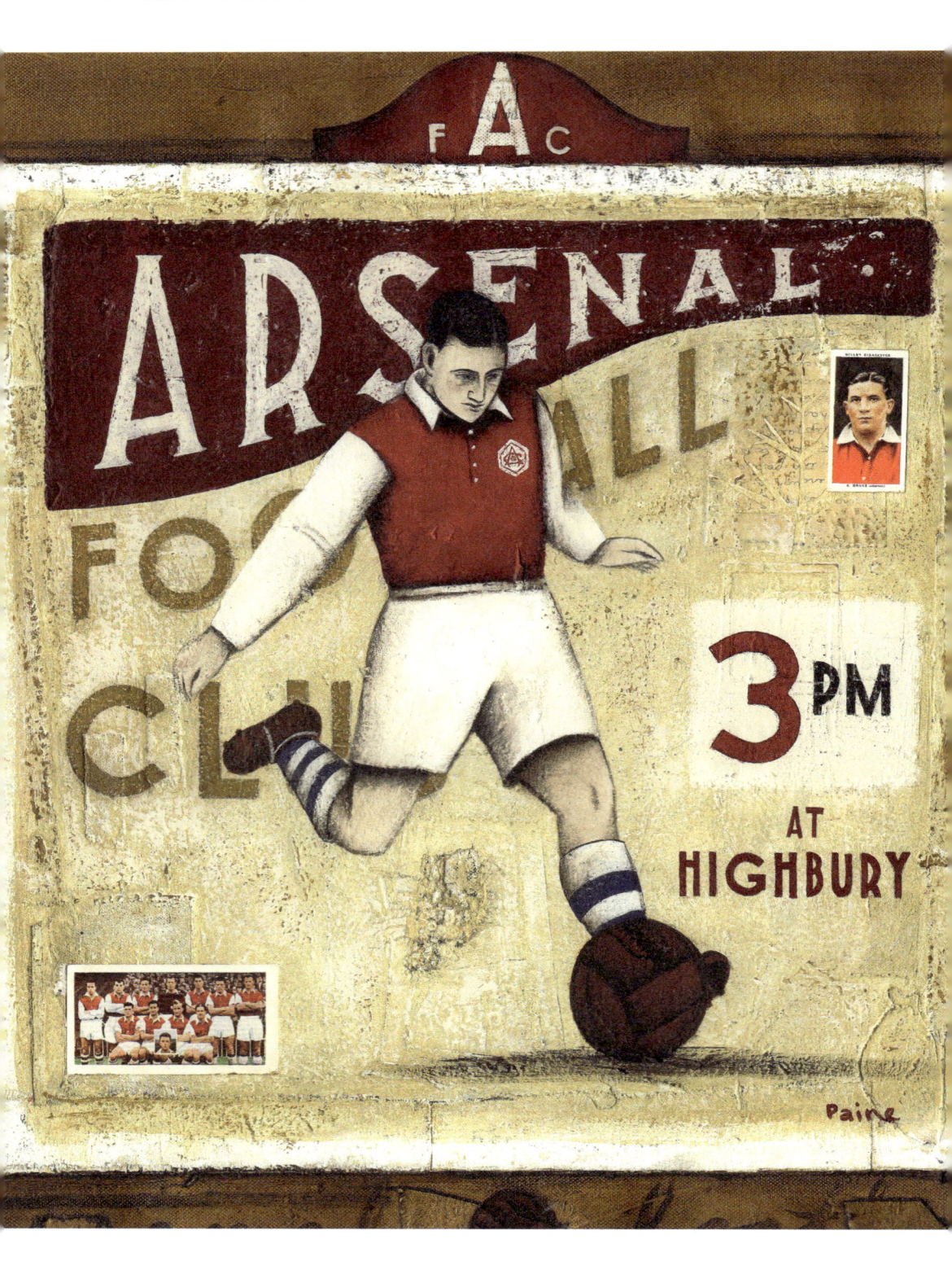

Earlier in the 1993/94 season, Match of the Day presenter Des Lynam expressed his disappointment that 'all' the English clubs had been knocked out of Europe, even though one still remained. A declining Arsenal team under George Graham were alive and kicking in Europe and managed to beat a tough Torino team in the quarter final. Then a 2-1 aggregate win over PSG took us to our first European final since 1980.

With a formidable Parma waiting for us; and Ian Wright suspended – the odds did not favour George Graham winning what would be his sixth major trophy for the club as manager. A 1-0 win was a major achievement, but the next day Des Lynam's question to new England manager Terry Venables was on the lines that: it was a good win for Arsenal but not in the style that you would want to win trophies. Venables didn't belittle Arsenal's achievement and was famously good friends with George Graham. But why can't pundits ever be happy that Arsenal has won?

**"JINGLE BELLS, JINGLE BELLS, JINGLE ALL THE WAY,
SANTA IS AN ARSENAL FAN, AND AT HIGHBURY TODAY - OH!"**
(Jingle Bells)

Santa wears red and white – what more evidence do you want.

**"JINGLE BELLS, JINGLE BELLS, JINGLE ALL THE WAY,
OH WHAT FUN IT IS TO SEE, THE ARSENAL WIN AWAY!"**
(Jingle Bells)

Xmas Gooners - A home and away Xmas song, sung heartily at White Hart Lane in 1978 during the 5-0 win. Alan Sunderland's hat-trick being overshadowed by a sumptuous Liam Brady curling shot.

**"WE'RE GOING TO WEMBLEY, WE'RE GOING TO WEMBLEY,
YOU'RE NOT, YOU'RE NOT!"**

One for a semi final, or indeed a quarter final these days!

"OLE, OLE OLE, OLE, OLE, OLE, OLE, OLE"

The number of Oles dependent on the number of passes strung together and the opponents

**"WE'RE ON THE MARCH WITH GEORGIE'S ARMY,
WE'RE NOT GOING TO WEMBLEY,
BUT WE DON'T GIVE A SHIT,
COS WE'LL WIN THE CHAMPIONSHIP,
COS THE ARSENAL ARE THE GREATEST FOOTBALL TEAM"**
(Ally's Tartan Army)

Sung with confidence just prior to the great 1989 victory.

WE'VE ONLY GOT ONE SONG

"WHEN SPRING TURNS TO SUMMER THE FIRST WEEK IN MAY,
YOU KNOW YOU WILL FIND US DOWN OL' WEMLBEY WAY,
IT'S A POPULAR PLACE AT THIS TIME OF THE YEAR,
'COS EVERYONE KNOWS THAT THE GUNNERS ARE HERE,

AND IT'S SUPER ARSENAL! SUPER ARSENAL FC!
AND WE'LL PLAY THE WORLD OVER,
AND CHAMPIONS WE'LL BE,

WITH A BIG MAN BEHIND YOU, YOU'RE SAFE AT THE BACK,
WITH SAMMY AND PAT MOVING INTO ATTACK,
THERE'S DAVID O'LEARY AND BIG WILLIE YOUNG,
SENDING RIXY AND STAPLETON OF ON A RUN,

AND IT'S SUPER ARSENAL...

WE'LL TAKE ON THE BEST OF THEM HOME OR AWAY,
AT THE END OF THE DAY THEY'LL HAVE NOTHING TO SAY,
WHEN THEY ASK YOU TO VOTE FOR THEIR MAN OF THE YEAR,
OUR OWN CHIPPY BRADY IS THE NAME THAT YOU'LL HEAR,

AND IT'S SUPER ARSENAL...

WE WENT UP TO CARDIFF ONE FINE DAY IN MAY,
WE HAD LOADS OF LAGER WHEN WE SAW THE REDS PLAY,
WHEN I WOKE IN THE MORNING IT WAS FEELING QUITE ILL,
BUT WE'D BEATEN THE CHELSEA BY 2 GOALS TO NIL,

AND IT'S SUPER ARSENAL...

WE WENT BACK TO CARDIFF ON ANOTHER DAY IN MAY,
WE HAD EVEN MORE LAGER WHEN WE SAW THE REDS PLAY,
WHEN I WOKE IN THE MORNING I WANTED SOME MORE,
'COS WE'D BEATEN MAN UNITED BY 5 GOALS TO 4,

AND IT'S SUPER ARSENAL...

WE WENT UP TO WEMBLEY ONE FINE DAY IN MAY,
AND ALL THE SUPPORTERS WERE HAPPY THAT DAY,
WHEN THAT DAY WAS OVER, WHEN THAT DAY WAS THROUGH,
WE'D BEATEN HULL CITY BY 3 GOALS TO 2,

AND IT'S SUPER ARSENAL..."

(The Wild Rover, with additional lyrics by Kelvin Meadows and Pete Glover)

This is an original official 1979 FA Cup song, that was updated for 2002, 2005 and 2014.

"SWEET CAROLINE!"
(Neil Diamond)

Sung rousingly at Wembley as it was played over the stadium speakers after the FA Cup final win in 2017. Personally Mark loves the song, but then again he likes Neil Diamond, though can see why many believe it has no place in football, and should remain as a summer cricket sing-a-long, rather than played at football matches.

**"EVERY SATURDAY WE FOLLOW, LONDON'S GREATEST TEAM,
UNAI EMERY'S ARMY, HERBERT CHAPMAN'S DREAM,
ALL ACROSS THE COUNTRY, AND IN EUROPE TOO,
WE FOLLOW THE GUNNERS, AND WE'RE ARSENAL THROUGH
AND THROUGH, ALLEZ, ALLEZ, ALLEZ, ... etc"**

For the Europa Cup quarter final against Napoli in April 2019 a bunch of youngsters in the Clock End premiered this song on the concourse. We believe it's a good indicator of the continued inventiveness on the terrace, as unlike those of us who grew up watching via terracing, they have no singing end or easy place to congregate together. So more of this is to be encouraged especially as they managed to reference Herbert Chapman into a contemporary song!

**"QUE SERÁ, SERÁ, WHATEVER WILL BE, WILL BE,
WE'RE GOING TO WEM-BER-LEY, QUE SERÁ, SERÁ."**
(Que Será, Será)

A timeless classic from the Doris Day songbook... one that has been heard in almost every football ground in the country at some stage, but most often at Arsenal, as we've won the most FA Cups!

**"WE'VE BEEN TO QARABAG AND EVERYWHERE,
SHAGGED BRASSES IN COLOGNE,
AND NOW WE'RE OFF TO BAKU,
TO BRING THE TROPHY HOME!"**
(Rotterdam or Anywhere)

The pre-final tongue in cheek song for 2019, that lost its sheen during the game as the few who were able to watch Arsenal in Baku witnessed a shocking performance. A fiasco aptly described by blogger and Arsenal writer Tim Stillman who was present noting the "grinding disappointment that was Arsenal's characteristic capitulation in Baku. As an experience, this was already the worst final I had ever attended before the team intervened with their usual brand of fuckwittery". Another European final that we did not show up at. Talking of showing up the quite disgraceful omission of Henrikh Mkhitaryan seemed to be studiously brushed under the carpet by the powers that be. An organisation that pays lip service to "Equality" and highlights a whole raft of pet causes every other week to show how politically correct they are. Yet when an actual and clear case of ethnic discrimination arose, which meant that a player was too worried to travel to the match with his club and by inference no one was able to guarantee his safety, nothing was seen to be done by the football authorities. And more worrying as an Arsenal fan, little overt action was seemingly done by the club to overcome this massive injustice.

PRE HIGHBURY

Arsenal's away support in their period at Woolwich was a potent mix of music, songs, chants, dancing, fireworks, drinking, pitch invasions and 'painting the town red'. It was similar at home less the fireworks and pitch invasions!

The Arsenal while at Plumstead were renowned for their musical and singing contributions particularly at away matches. They were fans who enjoyed a huge 'session' away from home. These Arsenal supporters had a lot in common with the old English misrule traditions, much like their ancestors had enjoyed the pre-industrial traditions of carnivals: namely drinking, inversion of the social order, territorialism, dancing and music.

"The Arsenal were accompanied by the most musically inclined lot of supporters I have met for a long time". Bristol Evening News 2 November 1901

"These Southern football crowds evidently believe in enjoying themselves when travelling, for nearly every saloon - there were 32 of them - contained some description of musical instrument". Yorkshire Sports 13 February 1904

Travelling Arsenal support when waiting for the match to start and in the interval would spend their time singing, playing musical instruments and dancing. Often they would be singing London football doggerel set to popular tunes. Especially true of this was the large away support, on occasion 3,000 fans, Woolwich Arsenal took to many away games in Nottingham, Bristol, Leicester, the Midlands and Bradford on their giant excursions.

There were many instruments taken to matches such as harmoniums, trombones, fiddles, concertinas and cornets. These instruments would provide the backing to those singing the 'topical airs', and would be played even louder during the game if Woolwich happened to score.

Dancing was prevalent on these trips, especially so were popular dances that appeared in Music Halls, and were copied by the revellers with differing levels of success. The cake walk was one such dance, it being an inventive couple dance where the two dancers would strut in a square to a lively tune. The walk was constantly updated on the Music Hall stages and these alterations appear to have been followed by the excursionists.

Unfortunately the football songs were reported stating the fans regularly sang, but rarely noting how each tune had been Arsenal-ised. So while some of the reports mentioned a specific Music Hall number they did not then print the new lyrics. Those reading at the time would have been familiar with the tune and words of the actual and altered song.

But we have been able to find a number of songs, aired both home and away which show the inventiveness of the Arsenal fan began many, many years ago.

"TA RA RA BOOM DE AY, THE ARSENAL'S WON TODAY
TA RA RA BOOM DE AY, THE ARSENAL'S WON TODAY "(repeat)
(Ta ra ra boom de ay)

First reported in February 1892, when many of the 3,000 Royal Arsenal fans chanted "Ta ra ra boom de ay, the Arsenal's won today" at local Kentish rivals Chatham. This is the earliest example of a terrace chant, revealed in the papers, specifically referring to the Arsenal team. A classic example of a terrace song derived from a music hall favourite, where the fans altered the original lyrics to celebrate their support of the Arsenal.

3-0 up just after half-time victory seemed to be in the bag so the Reds supporters sang persistent renditions of this song to taunt their opponent fans (hard to believe now but the Arsenal and Chatham rivalry was very real then). However, Chatham scored twice late on and the last few minutes were anxious for the away day faithful but the Arsenal managed to cling on to a 3-2 win. It's never been easy supporting Arsenal!

In 1891 while in the USA Lottie Collins heard this song, and once her husband obtained permission for use in England, she developed a burlesque dance to accompany it. The dance comprising stamina sapping can-can style kicks and the whole routine made her a Victorian music hall star. She performed it all over London through 1891 and 1892, and at the peak of the mania around Lottie it was said she enacted it five times a night in various music halls and theatres.

The song became a great crowd favourite, and was complemented with a terrace dance based upon Lottie's routine, all through 1892 and into 1893 at the home of the Reds, the Invicta Ground. We suggest you look up this song on YouTube to get an understanding of how well the song and dance routine works.

"GOD SAVE OUR GRACIOUS KING,
LONG LIVE OUR NOBLE KING,
GOD SAVE THE KING,
SEND HIM VICTORIOUS,
HAPPY AND GLORIOUS,
LONG TO REIGN OVER US,
GOD SAVE THE KING."
(National Anthem)

'God Save the King' is a patriotic song first publicly performed by the house band at the Theatre Royal, Drury Lane, London in 1745. The words and tune are anonymous and it became the National Anthem at the beginning of the nineteenth century.

The Manor Ground crowd, the majority being munitions workers and in the Army or navy, were heard on 9 Feb 1901 lustily singing "God save the King" assisted by a solo cornet player. This FA Cup first round tie against Blackburn which resulted in a 2-0 win, was the club's first home game in the Edwardian era, as Queen Victoria had died on 22 January 1901.

The Plumstead crowd were using this solemn tune to re-inforce their centrality to the Empire and its cause. It is not an exaggeration to point out that the Arsenal at Woolwich was the premier munitions plant in the whole of the British Empire, and to a large extent the workers and servicemen owed their living ensuring the upkeep of the colonies.

It could be the same cornet player who 10 years previously accompanied the triumphant Royal Arsenal team from the Oval back to Woolwich after gaining the London Senior Cup trophy by defeating the Old Westminsters' in 1891. He continually played the tune "IT'S ANOTHER COLOUR NOW" during the journey home, a reference to their beaten rivals and previous holders of this highly prized cup who wore pink shirts, whilst Arsenal wore red. This mockery was given added spice as there was bad feeling between the teams and their followers. Being an Old Boys' team they had a barely concealed distain for the working man's team – Royal Arsenal, and this was reciprocated by the Arsenal.

A Woolwich cornet was also heard playing solos during half-time at the inaugural League game at Stamford Bridge in November 1907 during the interval amongst the 65,000 crowd. The half time was a carnival atmosphere both Red and Blue fans swapping chants and songs with gusto.

At the conclusion of the 1937/38 season the crowd who had run on the pitch to celebrate Arsenal's fifth title in eight seasons sang the 'National Anthem' and 'Auld Lang Syne' before dispersing to the local pubs to continue their revelry.

**"PLAY UP, ARSENAL,
ARSENAL, PLAY UP!" (Repeat)**
(Westminster quarter chime)

This appears to have been the preferred chant or variant of chant from the turn of the century and especially during the halcyon years of Arsenal at Woolwich namely 1904-1908. A bit like the North Bank at Highbury, the Spion Kop at the Manor Ground was where most of the noise was generated in Plumstead matches.

Sung to the four notes of the quarter chime this chant was noted all through this period. It was often altered and during the 1905-06 FA cup run of that season where the club reached the Semi Finals for the first time the crowd were shouting and singing "PLAY UP, THE ARSENAL" and "PLAY UP, WOOLWICH" or "GOOD OLD, ARSENAL".

**"ARE WE DOWNHEARTED?
... NO, NO, NO, NO!"**
(Westminster quarter chime)

Another variation of the chimes was an extremely popular chant that followed the team home and away, usually away and was sung by two groups; those asking the question and those answering the question. Often it was sung if the team were losing! This was also used for important players where the names made it easy to fit into the tune:

"POP IT IN TIM!"
(Westminster quarter chime)

Star forward Tim Coleman (1902-1908) had the chant "POP IT IN, TIM". An apt chant as while at Woolwich Arsenal he was the club's top scorer during the Plumstead era, in fact his record of 84 goals lasted until May 1927 when Jimmy Brain overtook his tally. Coleman was a national figure who won the Military Medal in WW1.

"GOOD OLD PERCY"
(Westminster quarter chime)

Stalwart Percy Sands (1903-1919) was greeted with "GOOD OLD PERCY" in celebration of his ever dependable contributions at centre back. Captain between 1906-1915, only Tony Adams has been a longer serving captain of the Arsenal. Percy played 350 times, plus another 16 during WW1. He broke Roddy McEachrane's appearance record in April 1915 and held it until Alf Baker overhauled him in March 1931.

"WELL DONE RODDY"
(Westminster quarter chime)

Midfield dynamo Roddy McEachrane (1902-1915) had "WELL DONE, RODDY", in recognition of his indefatigable running. He had the honour of playing most times for the club in Plumstead, and eventually totalled 346 games which was a record until Percy Sands overtook him whilst at Highbury. If you think John Jenson took a long time to score, it was nothing compared to McEachrane who never scored for the Arsenal, even in friendlies!!

"DOWN 'EM JOHNNY"
(Westminster quarter chime)

John Dick (1898-1912) a very hard tackling centre half was encouraged to "DOWN 'EM JOHNNY" or "GO IT, JOHNNY" by the crowd. He was captain in the 1905-06 season and held the club appearance record between 1903 and 1907, eventually managing 284 games in total. Though his robust and forceful tackling did lead him suffering a number of long term injuries

"BRAVO BOBBY"
(Westminster quarter chime)

Enigmatic and popular right winger Robert Templeton (1904-1906) heard "BRAVO, BOBBY" whilst running up and down the sideline. He played in every round of the first FA cup run but left soon after the Semi Final, moving to play in Scotland for Celtic.

"PLAY THE GAME, REF"
(Westminster quarter chime)

"SET ABOUT THEM"
(Westminster quarter chime)

At home the Woolwich crowd had a reputation and would, game after game, continually Cry "PLAY THE GAME, REF" or "PLAY THE GAME, SPURS". Additionally using the quarter chimes they also, depending on the match situation, would chant "SET ABOUT, THEM". While they don't sound much today they were intended to be intimidating and in the case of the referee to criticise and "persuade" him to find for Arsenal in his decisions.

**"SAME OLD ARSENAL,
ALWAYS WINNING"**
(Westminster quarter chime)

**"SAME OLD ARSENAL,
TAKING THE PISS"**
(Westminster quarter chime)

The modern variant is still a crowd favourite and various versions albeit with differing lyrics are sung today depending on whether you are at the game supporting Arsenal or the opponents. Nowadays it may be: "Same old Arsenal, always winning", or if the team were toying with an opponent then: "Same old Arsenal, taking the piss".

However at the suspicion of unsporting behaviour by one of our players, the opponent fans will churn out: "SAME OLD ARSENAL, ALWAYS CHEATING". Many other clubs have used this tune as it allies itself to a number of different variants, probably the most famous being Portsmouth's - "PLAY UP POMPEY"

**"McGIBBON'S A JOLLY GOOD FELLOW,
AND SO SAY ALL OF US!" (repeat)**
(For he's a jolly good fellow)

In 1909/1910 Arsenal were involved in a relegation dogfight, not helped by the fact the club were liquidated during the season. Charles McGibbon (1905, 1910), a Sergeant in the Royal Artillery was drafted in as an amateur at centre forward for only four games near the end of that season. He scored in three of them, and it was his three goals for the team that saved the club from relegation in 1910.

This chant was heard being sung on the underground on the way back to Plumstead from Chelsea's ground after his solitary goal had given the Gunners a 1-0 win at the end of March 1910. Arsenal avoided relegation by two points, finishing one place above Chelsea who were demoted to the second division.

At Leicester, in April 1903 the Woolwich Gazette reporter was obviously nearby the action as he noted many songs, all humorous which was a difference to the norm, as the reporting at this time rarely mentioned specific songs. This is in effect a microcosm of away game songs.

These may have been Arsenal-ised and in many cases most probably were as if the support were altering songs as early as 1892 then they would not have stopped a decade later. But like so many working class pursuits there was very little additional information provided in newspapers.

These are examples of the intelligence in the Arsenal crowd, highlight the sense of humour as they picked out recent tunes for the situations encountered in the pre match entertainment. The concept of the crowd being their own entertainment was strong, unlike the sanitised ersatz pre-match climate within English football stadia today.

Ironically nearly all the tunes and songs originated in America which had made their way over to England. What follows are the Music Hall songs played by the Arsenal away band and "choir" and descriptions of how they came about to be played:

"IF YOU WANT TO GET A DRINK,
ASK A POLICEMAN,
HE'LL MANAGE IT I THINK,
WILL A POLICEMAN,
HE'LL PRODUCE THE FLOWING POT,
IF THE 'PUBS' ARE SHUT OR NOT,
HE COULD OPEN ALL THE LOT,
ASK A POLICEMAN!"

The band started this one up when the police, or Robert (after Robert Peel founder of the Police force) as they were colloquially referred to by the Woolwich crowd, arrived at the ground prior to the kick off.

Written in 1889 this song "ASK A POLICEMAN" had many verses and choruses with the above chorus being the most likely to appeal to the travelling Reds. While on the surface the whole song appeared to support the police the subliminal message was quite the opposite, especially after it was anglicised from the original American version.

> "FIFI:-WHEN WE ARE MARRIED,
> HARRY:-WHY WHAT WILL YOU DO?
> FIFI:-I'LL BE AS SWEET AS I CAN TO YOU,
> I WILL BE TENDER AND I WILL BE TRUE,
> WHEN I AM MARRIED, SWEETHEART, TO YOU!"

At the game a demure looking lady and her gentleman escort were greeted with the tune "WHEN WE ARE MARRIED", much to the confusion of the couple. Written in 1897 this US duet is sung between Harry and Fifi about their impending nuptials.

> "I CAN'T TELL WHY I LOVE YOU BUT I DO,
> THIS WORLD IS FULL OF MAIDS THE SAME AS YOU,
> BUT SOMETHING I CAN'T TELL,
> SEEMS TO HOLD ME IN ITS SPELL,
> I CAN'T TELL WHY I LOVE YOU BUT I DO!"

The entrance into the away crowd vicinity of a "plain and prosy looking lass" was the cue for the band to strike up the strains of "I CAN'T TELL WHY I LOVE YOU". A slightly cruel choice from the Arsenal boys. An American song originally written in 1900 it must have been a current favourite as when the band played it there were yells of delight, and not just from the Arsenal contingent, to greet the hit.

When a couple of ladies tastefully sporting colours of blue and white of Leicester appeared, instantly the band struck up "TWO LITTLE GIRLS IN BLUE" another US song from 1893. And the entry of the belated town band drew forth "OH LISTEN TO THE BAND" an English number from 1903.

Finally the Woolwich Arsenal team drew up in their vehicle and the band and whole Arsenal crowd began singing "THEY'RE ALL GOOD BOYS" to enthusiastically welcome the players onto the ground.

> "FAREWELL MY BLUEBELL, FAREWELL TO YOU!
> ONE MORE FOND LOOK INTO YOUR EYES SO BLUE,
> THROUGH CAMPFIRES GLEAMING,
> THROUGH SHOT AND SHELL,
> I'LL SOON BE COMING BACK TO MY BLUEBELL!"

This was notable due to the reds fans singing it almost non-stop during play as the songs were usually heard before or at the interval of games. In December 1904 Woolwich Arsenal recorded a 5-1 win at Notts County who were tenants of the Nottinghamshire Cricket Club. The away support were on fine form as with a fire-cracker accompaniment, the Arsenal crowd in the second half ceaselessly sang "BLUEBELL, FAREWELL TO YOU" which was a music hall number about a soldier, his lover Bluebell and war that had originated in America earlier that year.

CONCLUSION:
OUR VIEW ON THE CROWD EXPERIENCE

Mark stopped going in 1994 when seats were fully installed, and has only recently began going again. After being a regular since the 1980s Matt stopped going when the club left Highbury; disgusted over-expensive ticket prices and also disillusioned about the declining atmosphere.

In the appendices we have concentrated in parallel with the songs on the dilution of atmosphere from the mid 1990s onwards which has occurred for various reasons. We do not think the period before, especially the 1960s and 1970s, were a non-stop cacophony of singing for the hour before hand and then for the full 90 minutes every single game. But there is a difference between the crowd dynamics now which has reduced the experience both culturally and in spontaneity.

Both authors hope that in the future the atmosphere will come back and that the only way to achieve this is for a large area of the ground to incorporate safe standing (laws permitting) and for passionate and singing fans to be allowed to be together in the same sections. The atmosphere created in just one section will enhance the whole experience - and will also liven up the rest of the crowd and make them lose inhabitations. Football without a sing song just isn't the same!

The most insightful comment anyone ever made about support at the new stadium was on Twitter from long time Gooner - G @Northbank1968 (now going under the Twitter name of G@lowlife) who said:

"When I went to Highbury I went to see Arsenal... When I go to the Emirates I go to watch football".

He put succinctly into a few words; the shift away from a ground mainly full of a partisan local crowd, into a crowd looking for entertainment before a sporting contest.

And Tim Marshall, author of "Dirty Northern Bastards", carries on the theme in a concise account of the Ashburton experience, which is probably the most accurate ever put down on paper by a non-Gunner.

"Arsenal's stadium is one of those places where the club orders the stewards to tell everyone to sit down. A small but significant percentage of fans are either tourists, and so may think this is normal behaviour for a football fan, or are corporate class 'fans' who think they've paid to watch the game and so everyone else should jolly well sit down and watch it. From a few sections of the stadium you hear the die-hard 'Gooners' trying their best to create something from this hushed 'atmosphere lite', while in the away end you hear 5,000 people having their own party. No wonder Arsenal's support is better away than at home".

> "ARSENAL, ARSENAL, ARSENAL,
> ARSENAL, ARSENAL, ARSENAL,
> ARSENAL, ARSENAL, ARSENAL,
> ARSENAL, ARSENAL"
> (Stars and Stripes Forever)

The way this song is currently and rather monotonously sung at Ashburton Grove, lacks imagination and is overly repetitive, it is sung half-heartedly in the North Bank. The same song used to be sung with such energy and gusto.

Indeed after having this insipid experience in February 2016 against Hull in the FA Cup we decided to log every chant in the next FA cup and Premiership matches against Watford in March and April 2016. Additionally, we repeated the exercise a few years later in February 2019 to see if anything had altered. To that end, the lists and logs are contained in the Appendices, and doesn't really alter any of our preconceptions, nor probably yours, of the weakened vocal support in the Spaceship. Particularly so is an apparent reduction in singing between the two admittedly small samples over a few years.

However, while fan groups are trying to do something about the, at times, woeful vocal support at home the essence of what made a crowd dynamic has already been stripped away over a twenty year period.

The first stage was the Taylor Report with its obsession of making all stadia seating only venues at the highest level of football. Highbury was duly transformed, but fans could still at least sit together in groups, even if they were no longer able to stand where they fancied. This was not an Arsenal issue as the trigger was a political response to the Hillsborough tragedy. Arsenal had no choice as they were compelled to take this action.

Recent legal judgements have shown that the essence of the information around at the time of the Taylor Report was fundamentally flawed, so it will be interesting to see if any Football Club challenges the rulings. However this is unlikely as the all seater stadium is now firmly entrenched in the present culture, but it may allow a route to bring in safe standing.

Redaction, the fan group set up to improve stadium atmosphere, were moaning about the atmosphere at Highbury after the seats went in so it would appear that the installation of seats was the predominant event to halt atmosphere at Arsenal, but other events did compound the issue. Matt recalls the day it changed; the first game of the 1992/93 season against Norwich which was the first game after the demolition of the North Bank terrace. For the first time, there was a long and cold and morbid silence that wasn't there before.

Stage two was the introduction of the Jumbotron screens in Autumn of 1994 which were installed in the north west and south east of the stadium. By the next season there was a full pre-match 'entertainment' programme being shown. The prototype of the current pre match 'entertainment' was formed. Where the customer pays for 'entertainment', they are not anymore just a fan going to a sporting event.

Stage three was yet another dampener and occurred in the move to the new ground. The club dispersed many groups of Season Ticket holding friends away from their preferred locations which had the effect of creating silos of support, not a homogenous set of likeminded fans that stood on the North Bank or Clock End together.

However, while some believe the dispersal to be a conspiracy, it is more likely a cock-up by the club as they also managed to lose all season ticket records from Highbury in the process! Obviously if you are sat next to someone you don't know the chances of getting a song going are quite remote.

Sit down and shut up! That's pretty much the message that's come from stewarding since the 1990s. Pre-Taylor Report, stewards tended to be fans who celebrated the goals when they went in (check old YouTube footage, the fellas in the green jackets were stewards). They mostly had a good rapport with the fans and there was certainly no ill feeling towards them. What a contrast to now. The second a goal goes in, the orange bib army stands up and glares at the crowd, anticipating trouble. When a player runs up to the fans to celebrate a goal – the sea of orange bibs steam in like they're breaking up a fight They are reacting to orders of course, and most of the individuals who do these jobs are just hoping for a hassle free day and the wages aren't much to write home about.

Stewards seem to have been given three main purposes – to guide people to their seats – to make sure they stay seated - and then when the game is over to rudely tell fans to bugger off out the stadium (not that half the fan base would have experienced this considering they've already left before the final whistle). Over the past couple of decades fans have been chucked out for standing up and singing, or engaging with the away fans in banter in which has been taken exception to. The effect draconian stewarding has had on atmosphere has brought us to the point where fans are in two minds as to whether it is worth the hassle in getting chants going.

A further negative effect on the atmosphere was the club's effort to reduce old style fans influence and replace them with "tourists". Essentially a policy was enacted whereby overseas fans were preferred as they spent several hundred pounds on their trip to the ground as it was a one off. This policy has been admitted by marketing executives at the club and is a very real strategy.

Old school season ticket holders, or indeed old school fans will have their preferred match routine which is almost certain to not include spending shed loads at the Armoury or from club outlets within the ground. No, they would rather drink in their regular pub or eat at many of the local cafes like the excellent Piebury Corner.

Few of the tourists know the songs, they have no experience of being on a terrace in a crowd, which further reduces the potential to improve the atmosphere or quality of chants. By tourist we refer to someone who comes to a game once a season at best and that's it. It is not a geographical pejorative term. If you live in a foreign country and know the songs and have Arsenal in your veins, you're not a tourist fan; you're a Gooner.

Many seats have a fantastic view of the pitch but usually the atmosphere is awful. Seats are persistently either empty or the owner has sold to someone else. Hence, there is either no one there or a "tourist" with little knowledge of anything about Arsenal other than what they have been force fed from the club.

Their only reference point is what they have seen on TV or other seated arenas. How can they be expected to learn chants and songs other than a basic one based upon "Arsenal, Arsenal, Arsenal ..."?

The very loud sound system drowns out any fan intervention, allowing the club to feed what they want into the stadium setting agenda. At the aforementioned Hull game in 2016 the club repeatedly announced over the tannoy for fans to get to seats early for the "extravaganza" in the Barcelona Champions League game in 2016. Making out the event was fan inspired when in reality the fan is merely a cog in an attempt to push the concept of 'Arsenal London'.

The club always pushes its links as 'Arsenal, London' as, to not do, may see a move of tourists to other London clubs to hoover up their cash, as they buy their half and half scarves. Also with 10 minutes to go before kick-off "London Calling" blares out and try as we have - this song has little specific to do with the club, a bit like the "Wonder of You" beforehand.

One thing to note is the poor quality of tannoy in the North Bank Upper. It is very difficult to make out a lot of items that emanate from the sound system, indeed AISA, one of the supporters groups, has made this a campaigning theme with the intent to improve the quality for all the stadium.

There is little chance to generate an organic crowd orientated feeling before the start. In days gone by, the marching band was background noise which could be listened to if you wished or you could make your own entertainment by singing songs with your mates who stood next to you, or in your vicinity.

Indeed many would roar at half time or during pre-match to try to get the head of the Marching band to drop his twirling mace – now that is crowd entertainment! If he did drop it, the roar was even louder. Today's experience I feel like a prisoner to all-encompassing artificial imposed noise, for noise sake.

This is sad as Arsenal fans have a rich history of songs and chants going back well before the First World War to Woolwich.

In 1992 "Fever Pitch" by Nick Hornby was published at the time of the Arsenal bond being mooted and just before the bulldozers destroyed the terraces to erect stands in their place. "Fans worry that the end of terrace culture will mean the end of noise and atmosphere and all the things that make football memorable." This was a genuine concern of many at the time, containing much foresight and was noted by the author.

However the next sentence "...seats in themselves do not turn football grounds into churches" was not so prescient and shows how useful hindsight can be, as most evidence at Arsenal shows that their introduction together with other policies have adversely affected the atmosphere. Seats have improved views and comfort at the expense of the terrace atmosphere. Raw energy has given way to a relative calmness. The apparent dichotomy from circa 1993/1994 (first season all seated) does not mean that songs were any less inventive or intelligently put together after that date, but that the means by which the songs were pushed out to the rest of the crowd in the terraced years had gone. Hence the ability to congregate in likeminded groups began to erode with an all seating stadium. So while the quality of the invention of songs remained - the singing deteriorated most notably at home.

WHERE WE ARE NOW

In May 2019 Matt attended the Valencia Europa League Semi-Final and couldn't get his head round the flat atmosphere even though ten years earlier he had written a book about it, and so really should not have been shocked! Things had been on the decline since the seats were installed back in the early 1990s, but home leg semi-finals would still be red hot and passionate affairs. Things may not have been as good as before, but there would still be plenty of games where the crowd would roar and your voice got lost in the noise. Today, not only can you hear your own voice, but so can everyone around you to the point where you feel conspicuous. By 2019, and quite frankly ever since the move to Ashburton, things have simply turned rotten. Unless of course - fans staring at their phones and checking their email is now considered a great way to support your team. Most people just looked bored, or confused, as if they were not sure what they were doing at a football stadium. One woman had a little sleep on her bored looking partner's shoulder, which they could have done at home for free instead of paying 50 quid each. Fans filming themselves watching the game whilst giving analysis! Seriously – sort yourself out. Here's my analysis – support your team and get off facebook you ring-piece!

Fans leaving the first half on a whim with five minutes still to go – because drinking a plastic cup of overpriced piss in the concourse is the main reason for being there. Worst of all, fans leaving before the end in such an important game. This semi-final was the most important game in what had been another flat season. In the vital minutes near the end, the team were leading 2-1. A goal for Valencia swings it in their balance for the second leg. A goal for Arsenal swings it further our way. Everything is on the line, a chance to get to a major final, win a cup, and get into the Champions League. So naturally 25,000 to 30,000 people fucked off! The sight of red and white empty seats for all of Europe to see (well, the ones who bother watching the Europa League). Indeed, when this happened a month earlier against Napoli – Matt got asked why so many people left early by some Italian football fans who could not understand why this happened. The same fans who left are probably the ones who moan that the players don't show enough passion. Maybe, but what passion did you show – you couldn't even stay to the end of a semi-final. Aubameyang scored to make it 3-1 and only around 30,000 people were left to cheer it. Highbury held 38,000 by the end of its days – so we went to a 60,000 stadium so that only 30,000 people could stay till the end of a game! The crowd who were left then piped up and were loud for the final minute, in what was too little too late. Why could they have not made that noise 90 minutes earlier?

APPENDICES TO CROWD EXPERIENCE

APPENDIX ONE

Song and chant log, noted while sitting in the North Bank Upper: 13 March 2016

Arsenal v Watford - Quarter Final FA Cup.

Arsenal were looking to win to be able to go for an unprecedented modern hat-trick of FA Cup final wins. The only realistic hope for a trophy this season too.

Pre-Match
40 mins before tie starts.
Song blaring on tannoy.
Series of adverts 3-4 minutes.
Only crowd noise is Watford fans cheering players when they came out and again spontaneously a bit later.
Arsenal team got polite claps.
Only brief gap for 3 minutes from the incessant music (a non-organic noise) is the compere talking to mascots. Even that is stupidly loud.
More music instrumental I'm not aware of... And another stupid bland unknown song.
Another meaningless meandering semi-instrumental.
Adverts -Arsenal linked product for 4 minutes.
Teams read out.
Another semi-instrumental
Watford singing and making a noise briefly as teams leave warm ups.
Clash London Calling.
Watford again raise noise.
Compere brief announcement.
"We're the North Bank... We're the Clock End, Highbury" not from the crowd but piped via the sound system as part of the Video being beamed on the screens.
"RED ARMY" is the first Arsenal crowd noise – Just before teams walk out, from different individuals, no one else joining in.
Clock ticks just prior to teams walking out. Roar for team as both walk onto pitch. Players get big cheers as names read out.

First Half
"ARSENAL, ARSENAL, ARSENAL ..."
"WEMBLEY, WEMBLEY ..."
"WE'VE GOT MESUT OZIL ..." - Appears to have emanated from West Stand
"WHAT DO YOU THINK OF TOTTENHAM ... WE HATE TOTTENHAM"

WE'VE ONLY GOT ONE SONG

"RED ARMY" - Reprise. This chant is interspersed over the half, but never gets going properly.
"COME ON ARSENAL ..."
"WE LOVE YOU ARSENAL, WE DO ..."
20 mins gone Watford outsinging us
" OOH TO, OOH TO BE ... A GOONER"
" OSPINA AAAAH"
"COME ON ARSENAL ..." -Reprise
"COME ON ARSENAL ..." Reprise
"WE LOVE YOU ARSENAL, WE DO ..." - Reprise
"ALEXIS SANCHEZ, BABY ..."
"STAND UP IF YOU HATE TOTTENHAM ..."
"COME ON ARSENAL..." - Reprise.
Watford then reply "Come on Watford"
"WEMBLEY, WEMBLEY..." Reprise
"ARSENAL, ARSENAL, ARSENAL ..." Reprise
"COME ON ARSENAL ..." -Reprise
"WE'VE GOT MESUT OZIL ..." - Reprise, after a quality set up by Ozil for Elneny to shoot over the bar
"ARSENAL, ARSENAL, ARSENAL ..." Reprise

Half time
Adverts and Junior Gunners penalties
Arsenal ladies interview
Indeterminate song
Very few moments of quiet without a cacophony of noise over the tannoy
Players come out to "Jump Around"

Second half
"NA NA NA NA NA NA NA NA, GIROUD ..."
"ARSENAL, ARSENAL, ARSENAL ..." - Reprise
"WE LOVE YOU ARSENAL, WE DO ..." - Reprise
50 mins Watford score - they're having a great time. Watford crowd singing- "Que sera sera were going to Wembley"… and others.
"ARSENAL, ARSENAL, ARSENAL ..." Reprise
"COME ON ARSENAL ..." -Reprise
"COME ON ARSENAL ..." -Reprise
"DER DER DER DER DER, DANNY WELBECK" - and he's not even on the pitch just warming up!
Then Watford score a screamer in the 63rd minute.
"THANKS FOR THE MEMORIES, BUT FUCK OFF WENGER" - Shouted by a lone fan
"ARSENAL, ARSENAL, ARSENAL ..." Reprise
"ARSENAL, ARSENAL, ARSENAL ..." Reprise
"WENGER OUT" - Shouted by a lone fan.
Arsenal score in 88 minute - Welbeck
"DER, DER, DER, DER, DER, DANNY WELBECK ..." - Reprise

"ARSENAL, ARSENAL, ARSENAL ..." Reprise

13 songs or chants (not including the two Wenger related comments) in all for this game. Nearly all chants were being tried by lone or small groups, and had little success with them being taken up in the Stand as a whole. There was minimal whole North Bank involvement, except for "ARSENAL, ARSENAL, ARSENAL ..." and "COME ON ARSENAL ...", which were the pre-dominant chants heard in the North Bank on this match day.

APPENDIX TWO

Song and chant log, noted while sitting in the North Bank Upper: 2 April 2016

Arsenal v Watford – Premier League.

Arsenal's challenge for the title while not mathematically ended was fundamentally flawed, so the match didn't really hold too much importance from a playing perspective. What was important was the chance to commemorate Rocky.

I couldn't face listening to the pre-game assault on my senses, so got in as the game commenced and only noted the chants and songs.

First Half
"WE LOVE YOU ARSENAL, WE DO ..."
"ARSENAL, ARSENAL, ARSENAL ..."
"WE'RE THE NORTH BANK , HIGHBURY ..."
 "OH ROCKY, ROCKY, ROCKY, ROCKY, ROCKY, ROCKY, ROCASTLE"
"WHAT DO YOU THINK OF TOTTENHAM ... WE HATE TOTTENHAM"
Sanchez scores first goal.
"ALEXIS SANCHEZ, BABY ..."
"1-0 TO THE ARSENAL"
"OH ROCKY, ROCKY, ROCKY, ROCKY, ROCKY, ROCKY, ROCASTLE" - On the 7th Minute sung all around the ground for a full minute or so.
"BY FAR THE GREATEST TEAM ..."
"WE'VE GOT MESUT OZIL ..."
"RED ARMY ..." - Lasting for five minutes, with many more joining in than usual.
" 49, 49 UNDEFEATED ..."

Second half
"HECTOR BELLERIN NANANANANANA ..." Just after scoring the 3rd goal
"OOH TO, OOH TO BE ... A GOONER"
"WHO'S THAT TEAM WE CALL THE ARSENAL ..."

"DER, DER, DER, DER, DER, DANNY WELBECK ..."
"WE'RE THE NORTH BANK , HIGHBURY, WE'RE THE EAST STAND, HIGHBURY ..." - Twist on the classic
 "GOOD OLD ARSENAL ..."
 "GIVE US AN A, GIVE US AN R ... S E N A L ... THE ARSENAL ..."
" OSPINA AAAAH"
"WE'VE GOT MESUT OZIL ..." - Reprised on a number of occasions,
"ROCKY, ROCKY, ROCKY, ROCKY, ROCKY, ROCASTLE ..." -Reprised intermittently in the second half.

18 songs were tried, five more than the more crucial FA cup tie against the same team. Due mainly to the fact that the Rocky Rocastle memorial song was on the 7th minute and Arsenal played relatively well, winning 4-0. Hence the usually anxiety ridden "COME ON ARSENAL ..." was not heard, as it was not required. Of interest were the airing of the classics: "GIVE US AN A, GIVE US AN R ... S E N A L ... THE ARSENAL ..." and "GOOD OLD ARSENAL ...".

APPENDIX THREE

Thoughts on sitting in Sunderland East Stand seats as guest of the North East club: 24 April 2016.

Sunderland v Arsenal - Premier League.

In reality a run of the mill, end of season game for Arsenal, while Sunderland were in their perennial relegation dogfight.

Unlike at Arsenal there was no pre-match in the stadium build up except for a five minute classical intro just before the teams enter the pitch. This means you can think and is a much more pleasant experience than having your senses battered by white noise, as occurs at the Emirates.

Then just before kick off a quick 20 second burst of: "Wise men say, only fools rush in but I can't help falling in love with you", which as their club song very effectively raised the spirits and noise levels of home fans. There was a good SAFC crowd atmosphere

Conversely there was an awful Arsenal crowd atmosphere with very little singing or emotion. "SUPER SUPER JACK, SUPER JACKIE WILSHERE" the only one sung with any conviction.

APPENDIX FOUR

Song and chant log, noted while sitting in the North Bank Upper: 21 February 2019

Arsenal v BATE – Europa League Round of 32.

Arsenal's challenge for the Europa League took an unexpected turn when the first leg was lost 0-1. So this game had meaning as the Gunners had to win by at least two goals to proceed to the next round. The kick-off time of 5.55 had led to expectations of a very low crowd of 30,000, which was not borne out.

Owing to the awful pre-game experience this was first time I had ventured into my seat very early since the recorded game in March 2016.

Pre-Match
35 mins to go.
Very noisy indecipherable loud song. I can hear this outside ground!!!
Awful awful soul destroying dirge. While players warm up. And enjoy a 4-0 youth team win on screens.
Even worse song. Drowning out any attempt for peacefully watching or contemplating the team on the pitch. Is Ozil playing. Totally un-enjoyable this far. Just noise pollution.
More headache inducing loudness .
Little crowd. Hence no crowd pre-match interaction. And artificial club provided noise drowns out any chance of organic action.
Another in a line of joyless songs imposed unasked on the spectators.
Announcement. Respect.
Bate language announcement and team line ups for away fans. Minor applause from AFC fans for Hleb when on teamsheet.
London Calling only song to date where I can understand words. But distorted over sound system.
Good Old Arsenal. Only recognisable Arsenal music. Though not the original. An updated mash up. Still at least it's some progress.
Piped over the tannoy - "We're the North Bank. We're the Clock End, Highbury". Not the crowd.
 Some awful European dirge.
Clock ticks players out. Applause for teams. Reasonable considering ground half full.
Right here right now song accompanying the AFC team being announced. Biggest cheer for Ozil and Ramsey!!!
Announcer welcomes all specifically to the Arsenal stadium, interesting he doesn't say the Emirates.

First half
"RED ARMY ..."

WE'VE ONLY GOT ONE SONG

"ARSENAL, ARSENAL, ARSENAL ..."
"WE LOVE YOU ARSENAL, WE DO ..."
"WE'VE GOT MESUT OZIL ..."
Goal after 5 mins.
"1-0 TO THE ARSENAL"
"DER, DER, DER, DER, DER, DER, DER, DER, DER, ARSENAL"
"WHAT DO YOU THINK OF TOTTENHAM ... WE HATE TOTTENHAM" - Very weak and poorly sung rendition.
10-15 mins. Nothing from crowd then...
"COME ON ARSENAL ..."
"DER, DER, DER, DER, DER, DER, DER, DER, DER, ARSENAL" - Reprise
Arsenal, Arsenal, Arsenal - on screens when every corner won to encourage supporter participation.
"WE LOVE YOU ARSENAL, WE DO ..." - Reprise
"STAND UP IF YOU HATE TOTTENHAM ..." - In Clock End and West Stand, but not North Bank.
"WE LOVE YOU ARSENAL, WE DO ..." - Reprise
"RED ARMY ..." - Reprise
"DER, DER, DER, DER, DER, DER, DER, DER, DER, ARSENAL" - Reprise
"DER, DER, DER, DER, DER, DER, DER, DER, DER, ARSENAL" -Reprise
Then goal comes. 2-0.
"BY FAR THE GREATEST TEAM ..."
Not a bad feeling in the crowd as Arsenal have the aggregate lead now. But in the half there was no cohesive concerted singing.

Half time
A Euro dirge played as teams go to dressing rooms.
Adverts blare out. Lucky number.
More poisons to my ears.
At last some songs. September by Earth Wind & Fire and Lets Dance by David Bowie.
No Gunnersaurus or ex-player interview.
More Euro dirge before restart.

Second half
"OOH TO, OOH TO BE ... A GOONER" - Very, very, localised in small part of North Bank.
"ARSENAL, ARSENAL, ARSENAL ..." - Very short then longer when get a corner 50 & 55 mins
"RED ARMY..." - no take up, aside from the original chap chanting it.
Hleb gets surpringly big cheer when brought on
60 min. 3-0. Socratis.
"WE'VE GOT MESUT OZIL ..." - Reprise
"TORREIRA OH, OH, OH, OH ..." - As he came on as a sub.
"DER, DER, DER, DER, DER, DER, DER, DER, DER, ARSENAL" - Reprise
"WE'VE GOT MESUT OZIL ..." - Reprise, but only fleeting.
" ... & THE BOYS FROM THE LANE HAVE WON FUCK ALL AGAIN"

"RED ARMY ..." - Reprise
14 songs. Definitely a perception of a lessened crowd involvement than in the games logged in Appendix 1 and 2. However, the attendance of an estimated 45,000 when all in, was a lower figure than those two games from 2015/16. Despite the insipid lacklustre singing it was a decent fun atmosphere owing to the fact that the team quite easily got over the challenge of overturning the deficit. Most of the singing was fractured for the whole game, but a rendition of "BY FAR THE GREATEST TEAM ..." was the only song to take off during the game being sung by of the upper stand.

APPENDIX FIVE

Song and chant log, noted while sitting in the North Bank Upper: 24 Feb 2019

Arsenal v Southampton – Premier League.

Arsenal's challenge for the title while not mathematically ended was not on. So the match didn't really hold too much importance from a playing perspective, except that Southampton were threaned by relegation..

After a meeting with Matt before the game, I misjudged timings and got to the seat too early, so noted the shortened pre-game entertainment.

Pre-Match
20 mins to go
The aural assault starts with a terrible offering.
Carl Jenkinson gives young disabled players an award. Warm deserved applause despite crowd at only 20%.
Team line ups.
Emery pre match on screen. Sound system is so bad can't make out anything he's saying.
Some heavy metal
London Calling.
Good old Arsenal.
Piped over the tannoy - "We're the North Bank. We're the Clock End, Highbury"
Video with clock ticking and cannons at Woolwich barracks til players come out.
Mascots applauded off pitch.

First half
"RED ARMY ..."
"WHO'S THAT TEAM WE CALL THE ARSENAL ..."
6 mins early goal. Lacazette.
"DER, DER, DER, DER, DER, ALEX LACAZETTE..." - Strong version well sung.

WE'VE ONLY GOT ONE SONG

"1-0 TO THE ARSENAL"
"1-0 TO THE ARSENAL" - Reprise
"Oh when the Saints go marching in..." - Southampton.
"WHAT DO YOU THINK OF TOTTENHAM ... WE HATE TOTTENHAM"
Corner.
"ARSENAL, ARSENAL, ARSENAL ..."
"Same old Arsenal. Always cheating..." from Saints fans when Kolasinac was injured and the referee stopped the game during a Southampton attack.
"BY FAR THE GREATEST TEAM ..."
17 mins. 2-0 Mkhitaryan
"WE LOVE YOU ARSENAL, WE DO ..."
"WHO'S THAT TEAM WE CALL THE ARSENAL ..." - Reprise
"WE LOVE YOU ARSENAL, WE DO ..." - Reprise
"RED ARMY ..." - Reprise. Has a lot of take up in the Stand
"WE'RE THE NORTH BANK, HIGHBURY ..."
"ARSENAL, ARSENAL, ARSENAL ..." - Reprise. In response to a free kick outside their penalty area.
"WE FORGOT THAT YOU WERE HERE..." - In response to chants of "Southampton ..."
"TORREIRA OH, OH, OH, OH ..."
"OOH TO, OOH TO BE ... A GOONER"
"ARSENAL, ARSENAL, ARSENAL ..." - Reprise
"DER, DER, DER, DER, DER, DER, DER, DER, DER, ARSENAL"

Half time
Adverts
John Jensen interview
Health and Safety film.
Gunnersaurus penalties.
And for 10 mins no music. Wonderful.
Ball squad Junior Gunners advert and first half highlights.
No music at all - such a relief. Except for a 20 seconds instrumental when the players come out for the second half.

2nd half
"WE'VE GOT MESUT OZIL ..."
"RED ARMY ..." - Reprise
Yellows from saints met with "ARSENAL, ARSENAL, ARSENAL ...". Saints out singing afc with when the Saints go marching in..." and "Yellows". Southampton were the better team in the first 15 minutess of second half.
"Same old Arsenal always cheating" - Reprised
"ARSENAL, ARSENAL, ARSENAL ..." - Reprise
" 49, 49 UNDEFEATED ..."
"WE LOVE YOU ARSENAL, WE DO ..." - Reprise
Ramsey substituted for Ozil
"WE'VE GOT MESUT OZIL ..." - Reprise. Very weak.
"BY FAR THE GREATEST TEAM ..." - Reprise

"DER, DER, DER, DER, DER, ALEX LACAZETTE..." - Reprise on 75 minutes in an attempt to keep him on when Aubamayang is about to come on. It works as Iwobi is substituted, and not Lacazette!

"DER, DER, DER, DER, DER, ALEX LACAZETTE..." - Reprise
"COME ON ARSENAL ..." - Despite being 2-0 up the game is not over given the paucity of our play
"DER, DER, DER, DER, DER, DER, DER, DER, DER, ARSENAL" - Reprise
"WE'RE THE NORTH BANK, HIGHBURY, WE'RE THE CLOCK END, HIGHBURY ..." - Rare interaction between ends!!!

16 songs. No cohesive singing just groups and songs die out soon after starting. Only "RED ARMY..." and "DER, DER, DER, DER, DER, ALEX LACAZETTE..." chants get taken up properly. it was however the only game logged where there was chant interaction between the rival fans.

PostScript
Of course the atmosphere at some games is electric, especially the Tottenham and Manchester United home games of 2018/19, and had we chosen to study those games no doubt the intensity would have come through, but there would have only been one or two different songs & chants mentioned. This is because the repertoire is very samey, game after game. Which is not to say that some in the Upper North Bank don't try very hard to get the whole stand singing, because they do. But generally inertia wins.

SOURCES

Books and publications
Theatre of Silence: The Lost Soul of Football by Matthew Bazzell
Arsenal: The Complete Record by Josh James, Andy Kelly and Mark Andrews
Royal Arsenal Champions of the South by Mark Andrews, Andy Kelly &Tim Stillman
The End by Tom Watt
Steaming In by Colin Ward
The Bromley Boys by Dave Roberts
Fever Pitch by Nick Hornby
We all live in a Perry Groves World by Perry Groves
Fighting for Football by George Myerson
The Crowd at Woolwich Arsenal FC by Mark Andrews
True Storey by Peter Storey
71 Guns by David Tossell
George Armstrong on the Wing by Dave Seager and Jill Armstrong
The Romford Pele by Ray Parlour
Who's Who by Jeff Harris
The Complete Arsenal Record by Fred Ollier
Shall We Sing a Song For You? by Alex Shaw
Dirty Northern Bastards by Tim Marshall
Soccer History various issues
Gunflash various issues
Arsenal Progammes

WEBSITES

www.thearsenalhistory.com
www.weretheherd.com
www.blog.woolwicharsenal.co.uk
www.angryofislington.com
www.aclfarsenal.co.uk
www.onlinegooner.com
www.goonersworld.co.uk
www.gunnerstown.com
www.arsenal-mania.com
www.thehighburylibrary.blogspot.co.uk
www.reddit.com
www.royal.gov.uk
www.thearsenalcollective.com
www.soccer-history.co.uk

NEWSPAPERS & SHEET MUSIC

Daily Express, Daily Mirror, Sunday Times, The Times, Daily Telegraph, The Observer, Woolwich Gazette, Kentish Independent, Highbury and Islington Express, Various local papers from the British Newspaper Archive

When We Are Married by T. B. Harms & Co. Words by Hugh Morton. Music by Ousters Kerker, Ask A Policeman by Harding Bros. Composed by A. E. Durandeau, I Can't Tell Why I Love You, But I Do by Will. D. Cobb (lyricist); Gus. Edwards (composer), Blue Bell By Edward Madden and Theodore F. Morse.

SUPPORTERS ROLL OF HONOUR

Austin Meadows
Sam Meadows
Billy Meadows
Duncan Essex
Panos Papadimitriou
Keith Martin
Jack Harvey
Kelvin Meadows
Ian Beckett
Mark Rayner
Randy Botti
Marvin Gray
Roberto Puzzi
Rupert Ellis
Will Campbell
Michael Salmon
Phil Decatris
Sam Seabrooke
Jake Seabrooke
Jørn Brekke
Valerie Dennis
Barry Purchese
Andy Barnes
Mike Kavanagh
Mark Tavender
Damian Ferrari
Frances Cabral-Delaney
Dan Goldring
Martin Stepanek
Luke Sturtivant
Bernard Cherry
David Kilpatrick

John Arnoldsson
Joergen-Andreas Engnaes
Jon Gibbs
Nigel Evans
Alice Kerr
Jonathan Burgess
Vincent Lindsay
Chris 'Basher' Wainwright
Andy Tallentire
Paul Antino
David Calnon
Derek Alden
Greg Houghton
Stig Michelsen
Malc Fox
Nemanja Bulatovic
Robert Wheeler
Paul Fowler
Charlie Ashmore
Gary Lawrence
McKinley Lewis Morton
Paul Bezant
Patrick Meli
Jani Harju
Derek Speake
Liam Raby
Morten Berger Karlsen
Lee Murphy
Rob Taylor
John Mann
Marc Richardson
Wayne Anthony Davis

WE'VE ONLY GOT ONE SONG

Alex Gibson
Jane Roberts
Sean Power
Jonathan Cousens
Michael White
Ken Helie
Eric Huggins
Frank Stubbs
Stephen Naventi
Patrick Rainsford
Steve Kell
Sunil Patel
Simon Hunt
Valerie Hale
Gary Jones
Drew Dawson
Lucas Pinks
Richard Coulson
Jamie Mcweeney
Andrew Kelly
Chris Hopkins
Andy Selby
Mark Horner
Stephen Randall
Davy Boyd
Dean Goodman
Andreas Jalstrand
Ian Lawrence
Rob McNally
Mark Wilcox
Pavel Ghosh
David Blackbeard
Helge Olsen
Todd Grange
Marcus Papa
Ian Bailey
Gregory Phillips
John Justice
Chris Goodstone
James Loxdale

Liam Bush
Patricia Cleary
Andrew Steer-Smith
Keith Martin
Gro Thorsberg
Vinnie Glynn
Reg Reeve
Andrew Milroy
Simon Morris
Adam Whyte
Bernard Chaplin
Jo Denham
Patrick Ruane
Keith Gillett
Mark Rogers
Ian Colbourne
John Bland
Mike Kavanagh
Alan Gunner
Melvyn Kinear
Stephen Edwards
Steve Darling
Simon Hill
Alan Thompsett
Tony Waters
Martin Redford
Graham Stubbles
Chris Grove
Daniel Burrows
John Lawlor
Jake Green
Rob Waite
Ian Gordon
Stephen Pavelin
Steve Edwards
Gerard Fagbemi
Michael Joyce
Andy Monroe